# quickcook

# quickcook

tempting dishes served up in a trice

steven wheeler and matthew drennan

southwater

This edition is published by Southwater

Southwater is an imprint of Anness Publishing Ltd
Hermes House, 88–89 Blackfriars Road
London SE1 8HA
tel. 020 7401 2077; fax 020 7633 9499
www.southwaterbooks.com; info@anness.com

© Anness Publishing Ltd 1997, 2003

This edition distributed in the UK by The Manning
Partnership Ltd, 6 The Old Dairy, Melcombe Road
Bath BA2 3LR; tel. 01225 478 444; fax 01225 478 440
sales@manning-partnership.co.uk

This edition distributed in the USA and Canada by
National Book Network, 4720 Boston Way, Lanham
MD 20706; tel. 301 459 3366; fax 301 459 1705
www.nbnbooks.com

This edition distributed in Australia by Pan Macmillan
Australia, Level 18, St Martins Tower, 31 Market St
Sydney, NSW 2000; tel. 1300 135 113; fax 1300 135
103; customer.service@macmillan.com.au

This edition distributed in New Zealand by The Five
Mile Press (NZ) Ltd, PO Box 33–1071 Takapuna
Unit 11/101–111 Diana Drive, Glenfield, Auckland 10
tel. (09) 444 4144; fax (09) 444 4518
fivemilenz@xtra.co.nz

Previously published as *Hardly in the Kitchen*

10 9 8 7 6 5 4 3 2 1

*Publisher:* Joanna Lorenz
*Managing Editor:* Linda Fraser
*In-house Editor:* Anne Hildyard
*Designer:* Siân Keogh
*Photographers:* Edward Allwright, James Duncan,
Michelle Garrett, Amanda Heywood and Don Last
*Additional Recipes:* Maxine Clark, Christine France,
Shirley Gill, Carole Handslip, Sue Maggs, Annie Nichols,
Jenny Stacey and Liz Trigg
*Sylists:* Madeleine Brehaut, Hilary Guy and Fiona Tillett

NOTES

For all recipes, quantities are given in both metric and
imperial measures and, where appropriate, measures are
also given in standard cups and spoons. Follow one set,
but not a mixture, because they are not interchangeable.

Standard spoon and cup measures are level.
1 tsp = 5ml, 1 tbsp = 15ml, 1 cup = 250ml/8fl oz

Australian standard tablespoons are 20ml. Australian
readers should use 3 tsp in place of 1 tbsp for measuring
small quantities of gelatine, cornflour, salt, etc.

Medium (US large) eggs should be used unless
otherwise stated.

# CONTENTS

# INTRODUCTION

With just 20 minutes to spare, it is possible to serve good food that hasn't come straight out of the freezer. *Hardly in the Kitchen* shows how easy it can be to produce a delicious lunch or supper in less time than it takes to reheat a ready-made supermarket meal.

Although for many people fast food is necessary to fit in with their hectic lifestyles, fast food does not have to mean poor quality food. By mixing fresh produce with store cupboard or frozen ingredients in tasty and innovative ways, you'll be amazed at the dishes you can produce in no time at all. The recipes in this book, such as Avocado, Tomato and Mozzarella Pasta Salad with Pine Nuts, Oriental Vegetable Noodles, and Glazed Lamb, all emphasize clever ingredient combinations in order to maximize flavour, colour and texture and at the same time, minimize the effort needed in preparation.

A well-stocked store cupboard and freezer are essential when speed is of the essence, as are using fast cooking techniques and having a well organized kitchen. The introduction provides essential information on ways to plan ahead, on what constitutes basic store-cupboard ingredients and tips on sensible storage of food and equipment.

So, even on the most hectic of days, with good ingredients which are fresh, colourful and appealing and with the help of this inspiring book, you'll be able to turn a speedy meal into a spread fit for a gourmet.

**Planning ahead**

Getting organized enough to serve a tasty, satisfying meal day after day can become difficult. For many, thinking of something to eat is the first problem, and cooking after a hard day at work can often seem like a chore. To make it as simple and effortless as possible, it's worth doing a little forward planning.

Start off with a shopping list that includes store cupboard staples and fresh produce. Good raw ingredients are essential and

*Right: A colourful selection of fresh produce, including root vegetables, green vegetables and salad ingredients.*

*Below: Simple ingredients such as pasta, vegetables and cheese enlivened with fresh herbs make a quick and simple lunch or supper dish.*

need less preparation and less seasoning. Avoid foods that sacrifice flavour for convenience. Fresh herbs or herb butter (prepared beforehand) add interest to simple dishes. Look

for ready-washed vegetables to save time at home. Buy fish fillets that are already boned and skinned, and meat that is prepared for cooking. To enliven pasta and rice dishes,

keep in a stock of pesto and other flavoured sauces.

**Storage of foods**

When storing foods, separate sweet and savoury ingredients, except those that are used for both such as flour, eggs and sugar. Ingredients that are used often, including onions, garlic, olive oil and fruit make an attractive display in the kitchen if there is space.

All ingredients should be used up and replaced regularly. Spices should be bought in small quantities as they lose flavour after several months and nuts become rancid if kept too long. Remember to check regularly and discard any foods that have gone past their sell-by dates. With a well-stocked cupboard of basic foods in good condition, producing a tasty meal in 20 minutes or less, need not seem too daunting.

**Equipment**

A few good saucepans in various sizes and with tight-fitting lids are a must. Heavy-based and non-stick pans are best. A large non-stick frying pan is invaluable to the quick cook. The food cooks faster when spread over a wide surface area. A wok is an essential tool for stir-frying,

*Above: A wok is perfect for quick-cooking stir-fries and can also double as a steamer. Choose a heavy, non-stick wok for ease of cooking and save time washing up too.*

**Preparation**

When chopping vegetables, cut them to the same size for speedy cooking. Start vegetables which take longer to cook first so that all the vegetables are ready at the same time.

Freeze extra grated cheese or breadcrumbs, for later use.

Freeze stock in ice cube trays and use as required.

Stock the freezer with bread and frozen vegetables such as peas and broccoli, that do not require long cooking.

*Above: A bowl of strawberries, crème fraîche and a ready-made flan case are all you need for an impromptu treat.*

*Below: A delicious selection of fresh fruit is perfect for a quick snack.*

cooking food quickly and evenly in the minimum of oil, with no loss of nutrients. For efficiency, sharp knives save time and effort and are safer than blunt ones.

Use a food processor to take the hard work out of shredding, grating, blending, and mixing.

Lastly, for speed and optimum efficiency, keep your equipment to hand, especially those labour-saving gadgets that are most frequently used.

*Above: A good batterie de cuisine makes for efficiency in a kitchen where fast cooking is a priority.*

*Right: A heavy, non-stick frying pan allows food to spread over a large area and cook quickly and evenly.*

# Store Cupboard Ingredients

The following ingredients are shown left to right from the top shelf.

**Polenta**
Italian cornmeal. Serve with Gorgonzola cheese and salad.

**Flour**
All-purpose and self-raising flour are used for making white sauces and pancakes.

**Lentils**
Red lentils soften quickly for simple soups and sauces.

**Couscous**
Cracked wheat for tabbouleh-style salads.

**Sesame seeds**
Nutty and rich when toasted.

**Spices**
Cumin, coriander, fennel seed, cardamom and peppercorns are best when freshly ground.

**Pasta**
Use best quality fine vermicelli for soups, and spaghetti and other pasta shapes with sauces.

**Wild mushrooms**
Deeply flavoured dried ceps and morels come alive in hot water.

**Fresh herbs**
Parsley, thyme, garlic and rosemary add instant flavour.

**Long-grain and risotto rice**
Use white easy-cook rice as it has a good flavour.

**Almonds**
These provide a rich flavour in sauces and salsas.

**Buckwheat**
Robustly flavoured grain. Cook with couscous.

**Garlic in oil**
Garlic cloves keep their flavour in olive oil.

**Tarragon in vinegar**
Keep fresh tarragon in wine vinegar for year-round flavour.

**Pine nuts**
The intensely rich fruit of the pine cone. A great asset to vegetarian dishes.

**Stock cubes**
Good quality stock cubes are indispensable. Buy the additive-free type if you can.

**Cornflour**
This is used for thickening sauces and gravies.

**Capers**
The fairly sharp taste of capers makes an ideal accompaniment to meat dishes.

**Mustard**
A piquant addition to meats and savoury sauces.

**Green peppercorns**
Soft berries with an assertive heat. Delicious with pork.

**Pesto sauce**
Made from basil, garlic, pine nuts, cheese and olive oil. Use for speedy pasta dishes.

**Pasta sauce**
Make your own from a can of tomatoes. Serve with an Italian hard cheese.

**Canned vegetables**
Young vegetables are easy to serve with grilled meat and fish.

**Citrus fruits**
Bright oranges, lemons and limes offer fresh fruit flavours to savoury cooking.

**Onions**
Onions, like garlic and root ginger, add delicious flavour to a variety of dishes.

**Wine**
Sober judgment allows a measure of wine, as and when it pleases the cook!

**Oils**
Keep olive oil for flavour, and a variety such as groundnut for neutral taste.

**Vinegar**
Use a good white wine vinegar. Balsamic vinegar should be used only sparingly.

**Olives and pickled peppers**
These will provide a taste of the sun in the winter.

**Eggs**
Fast-food convenience in a shell. Properly fed hens lay the best and tastiest eggs.

# Dessert Store Cupboard Ingredients

The following ingredients are shown left to right from the centre shelf.

### Flour
Plain and self-raising flour can be used for fast sponges, tarts and easy pancakes.

### Caster sugar
This is a free-flow, fast-mix, easy-blend sugar suited to all good cakes and bakes.

### Icing sugar
This is powder-fine for easy icing and dusting. Sift before using to remove any lumps.

### Meringues
Store-bought meringues kept in an airtight jar can be used for impromptu puddings.

### Chocolate sauce
Make your own. Delicious with ice cream, sprinkled with toasted nuts.

### Cocoa powder
Use sugarless cocoa powder in drinks and desserts for a rich chocolate taste.

### Chocolate
Buy the best quality chocolate you can afford and store it at room temperature, never in the refrigerator.

### Cornflour
Use this combined half-and-half with flour for fine textured cakes and sponges.

### Citrus fruits
Oranges, lemons and limes offer zestful flavour. Heavy fruits offer the juiciest squeeze.

### Cherries
Enjoy these fresh in season, as they have a poor flavour when cooked. Choose sour, or buy ready-bottled for cooking.

### Melon
Fill your kitchen with the scent of a ripe melon. Serve cold with red berry fruit when in season.

### Bananas
Bananas are deliciously sweet when speckled brown.

### Pineapple
Pineapples are ripe when the skin smells sweet.

### Strawberries
Traditionally served with sugar and cream, but also ideal for use in hot and cold puddings, cakes and tarts.

### Pears
Partner pears with Parmesan, pecorino, Gorgonzola or Roquefort cheeses.

### Apples
Red, green and russet skins conceal a host of flavour. All these apples make a juicy and crisp addition to quick desserts.

### Peaches
Remove the skins from sun-ripened peaches by plunging in boiling water.

### Passion fruit
The sour, scented juice of this fruit is delicious when combined with strawberries and raspberries.

### Grapes
There are innumerable varieties of grapes available, and they can be red, green or seedless. Muscat grapes offer the best flavour and sweetness.

### Finger wafers
These and other ice cream accessories are a must for spur-of-the-moment desserts.

### Brown sugar
Less refined than white, brown sugars are rich in molasses. Dark sugars are stronger in taste.

### Flaked almonds
Uninteresting raw, a temptation when toasted. Scatter over ice cream, chocolate and summer fruit for the finishing touch.

### Ground almonds
Essential for moist cakes and sponges; substitute half flour with ground almonds in any baking recipe.

### Preserved fruit
Use canned or bottled apricots and raspberries for easy convenience in desserts.

### Eggs
Store and use eggs at room temperature.

# Crab and Egg Noodle Broth

This delicious broth is an ideal solution when you are hungry and time is short, and you need something fast, nutritious and filling.

## COOK'S TIP

Fresh or frozen crab meat has the best flavour. Avoid canned crab, as this tastes rather bland.

*Serves 4*

INGREDIENTS
75 g/3 oz fine egg noodles
25 g/1 oz/2 tbsp unsalted butter
1 small bunch spring onions, chopped
1 celery stick, sliced
1 medium carrot, peeled and cut
    into batons
1.2 litres/2 pints/5 cups chicken stock
60 ml/4 tbsp dry sherry
115 g/4 oz white crab meat, fresh
    or frozen
pinch of celery salt
pinch of cayenne pepper
10 ml/2 tsp lemon juice
1 small bunch coriander or flat-leaf
    parsley, to garnish

**1** Bring a large saucepan of salted water to the boil. Toss in the egg noodles and cook according to the instructions on the packet. Cool under cold running water and leave immersed in water until required.

**2** Heat the butter in another large pan, add the spring onions, celery and carrot, cover and soften the vegetables over a gentle heat for 3–4 minutes.

**3** Add the chicken stock and sherry, bring to the boil and simmer for a further 5 minutes.

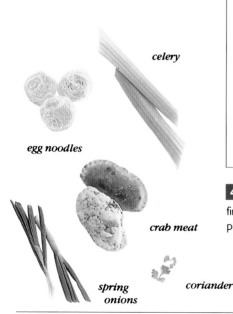

*celery*

*egg noodles*

*crab meat*

*spring onions*

*coriander*

**4** Flake the crab meat between your fingers onto a plate and remove any stray pieces of shell.

**5** Drain the noodles and add to the broth together with the crab meat. Season to taste with celery salt and cayenne pepper, and sharpen with the lemon juice. Return to a simmer.

**6** Ladle the broth into shallow soup plates, scatter with roughly chopped coriander or parsley and serve.

# Broccoli and Almond Soup

The creaminess of the toasted almonds combines perfectly with the slight bitterness of the taste of broccoli.

*Serves 4–6*

INGREDIENTS

50 g/2 oz/⅔ cup ground almonds
675 g/1½ lb broccoli
850 ml/1½ pints/3¾ cups vegetable
    stock or water
300 ml/½ pint/1¼ cups skimmed
    milk
salt and freshly ground black pepper

*ground almonds*

*skimmed milk*

*broccoli*

**1** Preheat the oven to 180°C/350°F/ Gas 4. Spread the ground almonds evenly on a baking sheet and toast in the oven for about 10 minutes, or until golden. Reserve ¼ of the almonds and set aside for the garnish.

**2** Cut the broccoli into small florets and steam for 6–7 minutes or until tender.

**3** Place the remaining toasted almonds, broccoli, stock or water and milk in a blender and blend until smooth. Season to taste.

**4** Reheat the soup and serve sprinkled with the reserved toasted almonds.

# Chicken Vermicelli Soup with Egg Shreds

This soup is very quick and easy – you can add all sorts of extra ingredients to vary the taste, using up any left-overs such as spring onions, mushrooms, prawns, chopped salami or herbs.

*Serves 4–6*

INGREDIENTS
3 large eggs
30 ml/2 tbsp chopped fresh coriander
  or parsley
1.5 litres/2½ pints/6¼ cups good
  chicken stock or canned consommé
100 g/4 oz/1 cup dried vermicelli or
  angel hair pasta
100 g/4 oz cooked chicken breast,
  sliced
salt and pepper

*vermicelli*

*eggs*       *chicken breast*

*coriander*

**1** First make the egg shreds. Whisk the eggs together in a small bowl and stir in the coriander or parsley.

## THAI CHICKEN SOUP

To make a Thai variation, use Chinese rice noodles instead of pasta. Stir 2.5 ml/ ½ tsp dried lemon grass, 2 small whole fresh chillies and 60 ml/4 tbsp coconut milk into the stock. Add four sliced spring onions and plenty of chopped fresh coriander.

**2** Heat a small non-stick frying pan (skillet) and pour in 2–3 tbsp egg, swirling to cover the base evenly. Cook until set. Repeat until all the mixture is used up.

**3** Roll each pancake up and slice thinly into shreds. Set aside.

**4** Bring the stock to the boil and add the pasta, breaking it up into short lengths. Cook for 3–5 minutes until the pasta is almost tender, then add the chicken, salt and pepper. Heat through for 2–3 minutes, then stir in the egg shreds. Serve immediately.

# French Onion Soup

In the time it takes to soften a few onions and brown some cheese on toast, this delicious soup appears on the table steaming hot and ready to eat. It makes a substantial starter or lunch dish.

*Serves 4*

INGREDIENTS
30 ml/2 tbsp vegetable oil
3 medium onions, sliced
900 ml/1½ pints/3¾ cups beef stock
4 slices French bread
butter, for spreading
115 g/4 oz/1 cup grated Gruyère,
  or Emmenthal cheese

*onions*

*cheese*

*French bread*

**1** Heat the vegetable oil in a large frying pan and brown the onions over a steady heat, taking care they do not burn.

**2** Transfer the browned onions to a large saucepan, cover with beef stock and simmer for 10 minutes.

**3** Preheat the grill to a moderate temperature and toast the French bread on both sides. Spread one side with butter and top with grated cheese. Ladle the soup into four flameproof dishes, float the cheesy crusts on top and grill until crispy and brown.

## COOK'S TIP

The flavour and richness of French onion soup will improve if the soup is kept chilled in the refrigerator for three to four days.

# Grilled Green Mussels with Cumin

Large green shelled mussels have a more distinctive flavour than the more common small black variety. Keep the empty shells to use as individual salt and pepper holders for fishy meals.

*Serves 4*

INGREDIENTS
45 ml/3 tbsp fresh parsley
45 ml/3 tbsp fresh coriander
1 garlic clove, crushed
pinch of ground cumin
25 g/1 oz/2 tbsp unsalted butter, softened
25 g/1 oz/3 tbsp brown breadcrumbs
freshly ground black pepper
12 green mussels or 24 small mussels on the half-shell
chopped fresh parsley, to garnish

*parsley*

*butter*

*garlic*

*bread*

*coriander*

*mussels*

**1** Chop the herbs finely.

**2** Beat the garlic, herbs, cumin and butter together with a wooden spoon.

**3** Stir in the breadcrumbs and freshly ground black pepper.

**4** Spoon a little of the mixture onto each mussel and grill for 2 minutes. Serve garnished with chopped fresh parsley.

# Deep-fried Florets with Tangy Thyme Mayonnaise

Cauliflower and broccoli make a sensational snack when coated in a beer batter and deep-fried. Serve with a tangy mayonnaise.

*Serves 2–3*

INGREDIENTS
175 g/6 oz cauliflower
175 g/6 oz broccoli
2 eggs, separated
30 ml/2 tbsp olive oil
250 ml/8 fl oz/1 cup beer
150 ml/5 oz/1¼ cups plain flour
pinch of salt
30 ml/2 tbsp shredded fresh basil
vegetable oil for deep-frying
150 ml/¼ pint/⅔ cup good quality
  mayonnaise
10 ml/2 tsp chopped fresh thyme
10 ml/2 tsp grated lemon rind
10 ml/2 tsp lemon juice
sea salt, for sprinkling

*basil*

*plain flour*

*eggs*

*mayonnaise*

*broccoli*

*beer*

*cauliflower*

*thyme*

*lemon*

**1** Break the cauliflower and broccoli into small florets, cutting large florets into smaller pieces. Set aside.

**2** Beat the egg yolks, olive oil, beer, flour and salt in a bowl. Strain the batter if necessary, to remove any lumps.

**3** Whisk the egg whites until stiff. Fold into the batter with the basil.

**4** Heat the oil for deep-frying to 180°C/350°F or until a cube of bread, when added to the oil, browns in 30–45 seconds. Dip the florets in the batter and deep-fry in batches for 2–3 minutes until the coating is golden and crisp. Drain on kitchen paper.

**5** Mix the mayonnaise, thyme, lemon rind and juice in a small bowl.

**6** Sprinkle the florets with sea salt. Serve with the thyme and lemon mayonnaise.

# Crispy "Seaweed" with Flaked Almonds

This popular starter in Chinese restaurants is in fact usually made not with seaweed but spring greens! It is easy to make at home and the result is delicious.

*Serves 4-6*

INGREDIENTS
450 g/1 lb spring greens
groundnut oil, for deep-frying
1.5 ml/¼ tsp sea salt flakes
5 ml/1 tsp caster sugar
50 g/2 oz/½ cup flaked
   almonds, toasted

*spring greens*

*almonds*

*groundnut oil*

*sea salt*

*sugar*

## COOK'S TIP
It is important to dry the spring greens thoroughly before deep-frying them, otherwise it will be difficult to achieve the desired crispness without destroying their vivid colour.

**1** Wash the spring greens under cold running water and pat well with kitchen paper to dry thoroughly. Remove and discard the thick white stalks from the spring greens.

**2** Lay several leaves on top of one another, roll up tightly and, using a sharp knife, slice as finely as possible into thread-like strips.

**3** Half-fill a wok with oil and heat to 180°C/350°F. Deep fry the spring greens in batches for about 1 minute until they darken and crisp. Remove each batch from the wok as soon as it is ready and drain on kitchen paper.

**4** Transfer the "seaweed" to a serving dish, sprinkle with the salt and sugar, then mix well. Garnish with the toasted flaked almonds scattered over.

# Hot Spicy Crab Claws

Crab claws are used to delicious effect in this quick starter based on an Indonesian dish called *Kepiting Pedas*.

### Serves 4

INGREDIENTS
12 fresh or frozen and thawed
  cooked crab claws
4 shallots, roughly chopped
2–4 fresh red chillies, seeded and
  roughly chopped
3 garlic cloves, roughly chopped
5 ml/1 tsp grated fresh
  root ginger
2.5 ml/½ tsp ground coriander
45 ml/3 tbsp groundnut oil
60 ml/4 tbsp water
10 ml/2 tsp sweet soy sauce
  (*kecap manis*)
10–15 ml/2–3 tsp lime juice
salt, to taste

*shallots*
*crab claws*

*sweet soy sauce*

*garlic*

*coriander*

*red chillies*
*groundnut oil*

*lime*

*ginger*

**1** Crack the crab claws with the back of a heavy knife to make eating easier. Set aside. In a mortar, pound the chopped shallots with the pestle until pulpy. Add the chillies, garlic, ginger and ground coriander and pound until the mixture forms a coarse paste.

**2** Heat the wok over a medium heat. Add the oil and swirl it around. When it is hot, stir in the chilli paste. Stir-fry for about 30 seconds. Increase the heat to high. Add the crab claws and stir-fry for another 3–4 minutes.

**3** Stir in the water, sweet soy sauce, lime juice and salt to taste. Continue to stir-fry for 1–2 minutes. Serve at once, garnished with fresh coriander. The crab claws are eaten with the fingers, so provide finger bowls.

### COOK'S TIP
If whole crab claws are unavailable look out for frozen ready-prepared crab claws. These are shelled with just the tip of the claw attached to the white meat. Stir fry for about two minutes until hot through.

# Butterfly Prawns

Use raw prawns if you can because the flavour will be better, but if you substitute cooked prawns, cut down the stir-fry cooking time by one third.

*Serves 4*

INGREDIENTS
2.5 cm/1 in piece root ginger
350 g/12 oz raw prawns, thawed if
  frozen
50 g/2 oz/½ cup raw peanuts, roughly
  chopped
45 ml/3 tbsp vegetable oil
1 clove garlic, crushed
1 red chilli, finely chopped
45 ml/3 tbsp smooth peanut butter
15 ml/1 tbsp fresh coriander, chopped
fresh coriander sprigs, to garnish

FOR THE DRESSING
150 ml/¼ pint/⅔ cup natural
  low-fat yogurt
5 cm/2 in piece cucumber, diced
salt and freshly ground black pepper

diced cucumber

peanuts

prawn

coriander

chilli

**1** To make the dressing, mix together the yogurt, cucumber and seasoning in a bowl, then leave to chill while preparing and cooking the prawns.

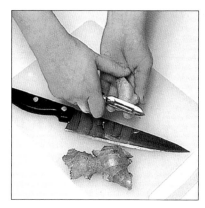

**2** Peel the ginger, and chop it finely.

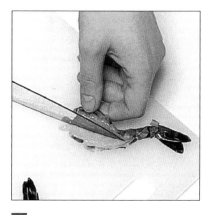

**3** Prepare the prawns by peeling off the shells, leaving the tails intact. Make a slit down the back of each prawn and remove the black vein, then slit the prawn completely down the back and open it out to make a 'butterfly'.

**4** Heat the wok and dry-fry the peanuts, stirring constantly until golden brown. Leave to cool. Wipe out the wok with kitchen towels.

**5** Heat the wok, add the oil and when hot add the ginger, garlic and chilli. Stir-fry for 2–3 minutes until the garlic is softened but not brown.

**6** Add the prawns, then increase the heat and stir-fry for 1–2 minutes until the prawns turn pink. Stir in the peanut butter and stir-fry for 2 minutes. Add the chopped coriander, then scatter in the peanuts. Garnish with coriander sprigs and serve with the cucumber dressing.

# Smoked Salmon Pancakes with Pesto and Pine Nuts

These simple pancakes take no more than 10–15 minutes to prepare and are perfect for a special occasion. Smoked salmon is delicious with fresh basil and combines well with toasted pine nuts and a spoonful of crème fraîche.

*Makes 12–16*

INGREDIENTS
120 ml/4 fl oz/½ cup milk
115 g/4 oz/1 cup self-raising flour
1 egg
30 ml/2 tbsp pesto sauce
vegetable oil, for frying
200 ml/7 fl oz/scant 1 cup crème fraîche
75 g/3 oz smoked salmon
15 g/½ oz/1 tbsp pine nuts, toasted
salt and freshly ground black pepper
12–16 fresh basil sprigs, to garnish

basil

pine nuts

crème fraîche

flour

pesto sauce

smoked salmon

**1** Pour half of the milk into a mixing bowl. Add the flour, egg, pesto sauce and seasoning and mix to a smooth batter.

**2** Add the remainder of the milk and stir until evenly blended.

**3** Heat the vegetable oil in a large frying pan. Spoon the pancake mixture into the heated oil in small heaps. Allow about 30 seconds for the pancakes to rise, then turn and cook briefly on the other side. Continue cooking the pancakes in batches until all the batter is used up.

**4** Arrange the pancakes on a serving plate and top each one with a spoonful of crème fraîche.

**5** Cut the salmon into 1 cm/½ in strips and place on top of each pancake.

## COOK'S TIP
If not serving immediately, cover the pancakes with a dish towel and keep warm in an oven preheated to 140°C/ 275°F/Gas 1.

**6** Scatter each pancake with pine nuts and garnish with a sprig of fresh basil.

# Chicken Goujons

Serve as a first course for eight people or as a filling main course for four. Delicious served with new baby potatoes and a green salad.

## Serves 8

INGREDIENTS
4 boned and skinned chicken breasts
175 g/6 oz/3 cups fresh breadcrumbs
5 ml/1 tsp ground coriander
10 ml/2 tsp ground paprika
2.5 ml/½ tsp ground cumin
45 ml/3 tbsp plain flour
2 eggs, beaten
oil, for deep-frying
salt and freshly ground black pepper
lemon slices, to garnish
sprigs of fresh coriander, to garnish

FOR THE DIP
300 ml/½ pint/1¼ cups Greek yogurt
30 ml/2 tbsp lemon juice
60 ml/4 tbsp chopped fresh coriander
60 ml/4 tbsp chopped fresh parsley

breadcrumbs

flour

eggs

lemon

Greek yogurt

coriander

parsley

chicken breast

**1** Divide the chicken breasts into two natural fillets. Place them between two sheets of clear film and, using a rolling pin, flatten each one to a thickness of 5 mm/¼ in.

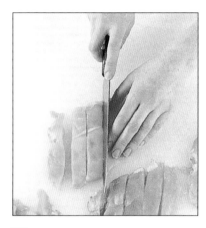

**2** Cut into diagonal 2.5 cm/1 in strips.

**3** Mix the breadcrumbs with the spices and seasoning. Toss the chicken fillet pieces (goujons) into the flour, keeping them separate.

**4** Dip the fillets into the beaten egg and then coat in the breadcrumb mixture.

**5** Thoroughly mix all the ingredients for the dip together, and season to taste. Chill until required.

**6** Heat the oil in a heavy-based pan. It is ready for deep-frying when a piece of bread tossed into the oil sizzles on the surface. Fry the goujons in batches until golden and crisp. Drain on kitchen paper and keep warm in the oven until all the chicken has been fried. Garnish with lemon slices and sprigs of fresh coriander.

## Filled Croissants

Croissants are very versatile and can be used with sweet or savoury fillings.

### Makes 2

INGREDIENTS
2 croissants
knob of butter
2 eggs
salt and pepper
1 tablespoon double (heavy) cream
50 g/2 oz smoked salmon, chopped
1 sprig fresh dill, to garnish

*croissants*

*smoked salmon*

*eggs*

**1** Preheat the oven to 180°C/350°F/gas mark 4. Slice the croissants in half horizontally and warm in the oven for 5–6 minutes.

**2** Melt a knob of butter in a small pan. Beat the eggs in a bowl with seasoning to taste.

**3** Add the eggs to the pan and cook for 2 minutes, stirring constantly.

**4** Remove from the heat and stir in the cream and smoked salmon.

**5** Spoon the smoked salmon mixture into the warmed croissants and garnish.

## PEAR AND STILTON FILLING

Soften 100 g/4 oz Stilton cheese with a fork and mix in 1 peeled, cored and chopped ripe pear and 15 ml/1 tbsp chopped chives with a little black pepper. Spoon into a split croissant and bake in a preheated oven for 5 minutes.

# Soufflé Omelette

This delectable soufflé omlette is light and delicate enough to melt in the mouth.

*Serves 1*

INGREDIENTS
2 eggs, separated
30 ml/2 tbsp cold water
15 ml/1 tbsp chopped fresh coriander
salt and freshly ground black pepper
7.5 ml/½ tbsp olive oil
30 ml/2 tbsp mango chutney
25 g/1 oz/¼ cup Jarlsberg cheese, grated

*Jarlsberg*

*mango chutney*

*eggs*

*coriander*

## COOK'S TIP

A light hand is essential to the success of this dish. Do not overmix the egg whites into the yolks or the mixture will be heavy.

**1** Beat the egg yolks together with the cold water, coriander and seasoning.

**2** Whisk the egg whites until stiff but not dry and gently fold into the egg yolk mixture.

**3** Heat the oil in a frying pan, pour in the egg mixture and reduce the heat. Do not stir. Cook until the omelette becomes puffy and golden brown on the underside (carefully lift one edge with a palette knife to check).

**4** Spoon on the chutney and sprinkle on the Jarlsberg. Fold over and slide onto a warm plate. Eat immediately. (If preferred, before adding the chutney and cheese, place the pan under a hot grill to set the top.)

# Fritters

A variation on beef patties, coated in batter and lightly fried, this tasty alternative need only be served with a light salad to provide a substantial snack.

*Serves 4*

INGREDIENTS
FOR THE PATTIES
225 g/8 oz/2 cups minced beef
1 onion, grated
10 ml/2 tsp chopped fresh oregano
50 g/2 oz/½ cup canned sweetcorn, drained
5 ml/1 tsp mustard
115 g/4 oz/2 cups fresh white breadcrumbs
oil for deep-frying
salt and freshly ground black pepper

FOR THE BATTER
115 g/4 oz/1 cup plain flour
60 ml/2 fl oz/¼ cup warm water
40 g/1½ oz/3 tbsp melted butter
60 ml/2 fl oz/¼ cup cold water
1 egg white

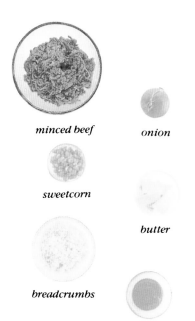

*minced beef*    *onion*

*sweetcorn*

*butter*

*breadcrumbs*

*oregano*

*mustard*

**1** For the patties, place the minced beef in a bowl and mash with a fork. Add the onion, oregano, sweetcorn, mustard and breadcrumbs. Season well.

**2** Form into eight round patties with lightly floured hands.

**3** For the batter, sift the flour into a bowl and stir in the warm water and melted butter. Mix to a smooth batter with the cold water. Whisk the egg white until peaking and fold into the mixture.

**4** Heat the oil for deep-frying to 160°C/325°F. Dip the patties into the batter to coat and fry two at a time in the oil. Drain on absorbent kitchen paper and serve with tomato pickle and green salad.

# Tomato Omelette Envelopes

Delicious chive omelettes, folded and filled with tomato and melting Camembert cheese.

## Serves 2

INGREDIENTS
1 small onion
4 tomatoes
30 ml/2 tbsp vegetable oil
4 eggs
30 ml/2 tbsp snipped fresh chives
115 g/4 oz Camembert cheese,
  rinded and diced
salt and freshly ground black pepper

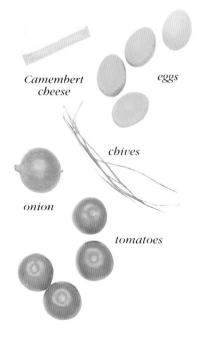

*Camembert cheese*

*eggs*

*chives*

*onion*

*tomatoes*

**1** Cut the onion in half. Cut each half into thin wedges. Cut the tomatoes into wedges of similar size.

**2** Heat 15 ml/1 tbsp of the oil in a frying pan. Cook the onion for 2 minutes over a moderate heat, then raise the heat and add the tomatoes. Cook for a further 2 minutes, then remove the pan from the heat.

**3** Beat the eggs with the chives in a bowl. Add salt and pepper to taste. Heat the remaining oil in an omelette pan. Add half the egg mixture and tilt the pan to spread thinly. Cook for 1 minute.

**4** Flip the omelette over and cook for 1 minute more. Remove from the pan and keep hot. Make a second omelette with the remaining egg mixture.

**5** Return the tomato mixture to a high heat. Add the cheese and toss the mixture over the heat for 1 minute.

**6** Divide the mixture between the omelettes and fold them over. Serve at once. Add crisp lettuce leaves and chunks of Granary bread, if liked.

## COOK'S TIP
You may need to wipe the pan clean between the omelettes and reheat a little more oil.

# Croque Monsieur

Probably the most popular snack food in France, this hot cheese and ham sandwich can be either fried or grilled.

### Makes 2

INGREDIENTS
4 slices white bread
25 g/1 oz/2 tbsp softened butter
2 thin slices lean ham
50 g/2 oz Gruyère cheese,
  thinly sliced
1 sprig flat leaf parsley, to garnish

*white bread*

*Gruyère cheese*

*ham*

## COOK'S TIP

A flavoured butter can be used to complement a sandwich filling – for example, horseradish butter with beef, mustard butter with ham, lemon and dill butter with fish. To make these just beat the chosen flavouring into the softened butter with some seasoning. Other useful flavourings for butter are: anchovy or curry paste, garlic, herbs, Tabasco or chilli. These butters can also be used in open sandwiches.

**1** Spread the bread with butter.

**2** Lay the ham on 2 of the buttered sides of bread.

**3** Lay the Gruyère cheese slices on top of the ham and sandwich with the buttered bread slices. Press firmly together and cut off the crusts.

**4** Spread the top with butter, place on a rack and cook for 2½ minutes under the grill preheated to a low to moderate temperature.

**5** Turn the sandwiches over, spread the remaining butter over the top and return to the grill for a further 2½ minutes, until the bread is golden brown and the cheese is beginning to melt. Garnish with a sprig of flat leaf parsley.

# Sardines with Warm Herb Salsa

Plain grilling is the very best way to cook fresh sardines; served with this luscious herb salsa the only other essential item is fresh, crusty bread, to mop up the tasty juices.

*Serves 4*

12–16 fresh sardines
oil for brushing
juice of 1 lemon

FOR THE SALSA
15 ml/1 tbsp butter
4 spring onions, chopped
1 garlic clove, finely chopped
30 ml/2 tbsp finely chopped
    fresh parsley
30 ml/2 tbsp finely snipped
    fresh chives
30 ml/2 tbsp finely chopped
    fresh basil
30 ml/2 tbsp green olive paste
10 ml/2 tsp balsamic vinegar
rind of 1 lemon
salt and freshly ground black
    pepper

*sardines*

*butter*

*green olive paste*

*balsamic vinegar*

*lemon*

*spring onions*

*parsley*

*basil*      *chives*

**1** To clean the sardines, use small scissors to slit them along the belly and pull out the innards. Wipe the fish with kitchen paper and then arrange on a grill rack.

**2** Melt the butter and gently sauté the spring onions and garlic for about 2 minutes, shaking the pan occasionally, until softened but not browned.

**3** Add the lemon rind and remaining ingredients and keep warm on the edge of the barbecue. Do not allow to boil.

**4** Brush the sardines lightly with oil and sprinkle with lemon juice, salt and pepper. Cook for about 2 minutes on each side, over a moderate heat. Serve with the warm salsa and crusty bread.

# Chilli Beef Tacos

A taco is a soft wheat or corn tortilla wrapped around a spicy warm savoury filling – you could describe it as a Mexican sandwich.

## Makes 4

INGREDIENTS
15 ml/1 tbsp oil
1 small onion, chopped
2 garlic cloves, chopped
175 g/6 oz/¾ cup minced
   beef
7 ml/½ tbsp flour
200 g/7 oz can tomatoes
7 ml/½ tbsp Jalapeño peppers, finely
   chopped
salt
4 wheat or corn tortillas
45 ml/3 tbsp soured cream
½ avocado, peeled, stoned
   and sliced
1 tomato, sliced
Tomato Salsa, to serve (optional)

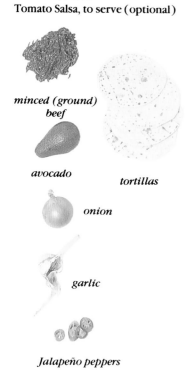

*minced (ground) beef*

*avocado*

*tortillas*

*onion*

*garlic*

*Jalapeño peppers*

**1** Heat the oil in a frying-pan (skillet), add the onion and fry until softened. Add the garlic and beef and cook, stirring so that the meat is broken up as it seals.

**2** Stir in the flour, then add the canned tomatoes, peppers and salt to taste.

**3** Heat the tortillas one at a time in a medium-hot lightly oiled pan.

**4** Spread a spoonful of the meat mixture over each tortilla.

**5** Top each tortilla with some soured cream and avocado and tomato slices. Roll up and eat immediately with Tomato Salsa if liked.

# Tostadas with Refried Beans

A tostada is a crisp, fried tortilla used as a base on which to pile the topping of your choice – a variation on a sandwich and a very tasty snack popular in Mexico and South America.

*Makes 6*

INGREDIENTS
30 ml/2 tbsp oil
1 onion, chopped
2 garlic cloves, chopped
2.5 ml/½ tsp chilli powder
425 g/15 oz can borlotti or pinto
  beans, drained
150 ml/5 fl oz/⅔ cup chicken stock
15 ml/1 tbsp tomato purée
30 ml/2 tbsp chopped fresh coriander
salt and pepper
6 wheat or corn tortillas
45 ml/3 tbsp Tomato Salsa
30 ml/2 tbsp soured cream
50 g/2 oz/½ cup grated Cheddar
  cheese
fresh coriander leaves, to garnish

beans

onion

tortillas

garlic

chilli powder

tomato purée

Cheddar cheese    coriander

**1** Heat the oil in a pan and fry the onion until softened.

**2** Add the garlic and chilli powder and fry for 1 minute, stirring.

**3** Mix in the beans and mash very roughly with a potato masher.

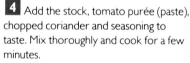

**4** Add the stock, tomato purée (paste), chopped coriander and seasoning to taste. Mix thoroughly and cook for a few minutes.

**5** Fry the tortillas in hot oil for 1 minute, turning once, until crisp, then drain on kitchen paper.

## TOMATO SALSA

Makes about 300 ml/10 fl oz/1¼ cups

1 small onion, chopped
1 garlic clove, crushed
2 fresh green chillies, seeded and
  finely chopped, or 5 ml/1 tsp
  bottled chopped chillies
450 g/1 lb tomatoes, skinned and
  chopped
salt
30 ml/2 tbsp chopped fresh coriander

Stir all the ingredients together until
well mixed.

**6** Put a spoonful of refried beans on
each tostada, spoon over some Tomato
Salsa, then some soured cream, sprinkle
with grated Cheddar cheese and garnish
with coriander.

# Deep-fried Whitebait

A spicy coating on these fish gives this favourite dish a crunchy bite.

## Serves 6

### INGREDIENTS
115 g/4 oz/1 cup plain flour
2.5 ml/ ½ tsp curry powder
2.5 ml/ ½ tsp ground ginger
2.5 ml/ ½ tsp ground cayenne pepper
pinch of salt
1.1 kg/2½ lb fresh or frozen
   whitebait, thawed
vegetable oil for deep-frying
lemon wedges, to garnish

*cayenne pepper*

*ground ginger*

*curry powder*

*lemon*

*whitebait*

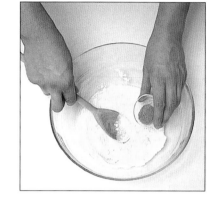

**1** Mix together all the dry ingredients in a large bowl.

**2** Coat the fish in the flour.

**3** Heat the oil in a large, heavy-based saucepan until it reaches a temperature of 190°C/375°F. Fry the whitebait in batches for 2–3 minutes until the fish is golden and crispy.

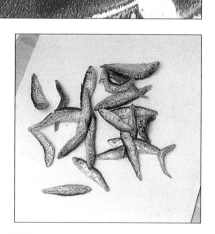

**4** Drain well on absorbent kitchen paper. Serve hot garnished with lemon wedges.

# Spiced Chicken Livers

Chicken livers can be bought frozen, but make sure that you defrost them thoroughly before using. Serve as a first course or light meal along with a mixed salad and garlic bread.

*Serves 4*

INGREDIENTS
350 g/12 oz chicken livers
115 g/4 oz/1 cup plain flour
2.5 ml/½ tsp ground coriander
2.5 ml/½ tsp ground cumin
2.5 ml/½ tsp ground cardamom seeds
1.25 ml/¼ tsp ground paprika
1.25 ml/¼ tsp ground nutmeg
90 ml/6 tbsp olive oil
salt and freshly ground black pepper
garlic bread, to serve

*chicken livers*

*olive oil*

*flour*

*coriander*

*cardamom seeds*

*cumin*

*paprika*

*nutmeg*

**1** Dry the chicken livers on paper towels, removing any unwanted pieces. Cut the large livers in half and leave the smaller ones whole.

**2** Mix the flour with all the spices and the seasoning.

**3** Coat the first batch of livers with spiced flour, separating each piece. Heat the oil in a large frying pan and fry the livers in small batches. (This helps to keep the oil temperature high and prevents the flour from becoming soggy.)

**4** Fry quickly, stirring frequently, until crispy. Keep warm and repeat with the remaining livers. Serve immediately with warm garlic bread.

# Cucumber and Alfalfa Tortillas

Wheat tortillas are extremely simple to prepare at home. Served with a crisp, fresh salsa, they make a marvellous light lunch or supper dish.

## COOK'S TIP

When peeling the avocado be sure to scrape off the bright green flesh from immediately under the skin as this gives the sauce its vivid green colour.

*Serves 4*

INGREDIENTS
225 g/8 oz/2 cups plain flour
pinch of salt
45 ml/3 tbsp olive oil
100 ml–150 ml/4–5 fl oz/½–⅔ cup
   warm water
lime wedges, to garnish

FOR THE SALSA
1 red onion, finely chopped
1 fresh red chilli, seeded and finely
   chopped
30 ml/2 tbsp chopped fresh dill or
   coriander
½ cucumber, peeled and chopped
175 g/6 oz alfalfa sprouts

FOR THE SAUCE
1 large avocado, peeled and stoned
juice of 1 lime
25 g/1 oz/2 tbsp soft goat's cheese
pinch of paprika

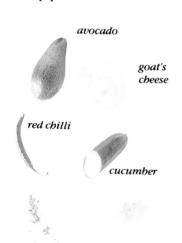

*avocado*

*goat's cheese*

*red chilli*

*cucumber*

*dill*          *alfalfa sprouts*

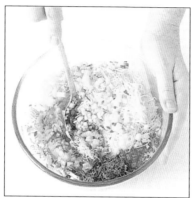

**1** Mix all the salsa ingredients together in a bowl and set aside.

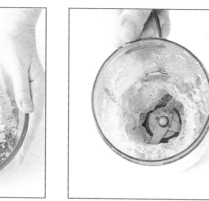

**2** To make the sauce, place the avocado, lime juice and goat's cheese in a food processor or blender and blend until smooth. Place in a bowl and cover with clear film. Dust with paprika just before serving.

**3** To make the tortillas, place the flour and salt in a food processor, add the oil and blend. Gradually add the water (the amount will vary depending on the type of flour). Stop adding water when a stiff dough has formed. Turn out onto a floured board and knead until smooth. Cover with a damp cloth.

**4** Divide the mixture into 8 pieces. Knead each piece for a couple of minutes and form into a ball. Flatten and roll out each ball to a 23 cm/9 in circle.

**5** Heat an ungreased heavy-based pan. Cook 1 tortilla at a time for about 30 seconds on each side. Place the cooked tortillas in a clean tea-towel and repeat until you have 8 tortillas.

**6** To serve, spread each tortilla with a spoonful of avocado sauce, top with salsa and roll up. Garnish with lime wedges.

# Stilton Burger

Slightly more up-market than the traditional burger, this tasty recipe contains a delicious surprise. The lightly melted Stilton cheese encased in a crunchy burger is absolutely delicious.

*Serves 4*

### INGREDIENTS

450 g/1 lb/4 cups minced beef
1 onion, finely chopped
1 celery stick, chopped
5 ml/1 tsp dried mixed herbs
5 ml/1 tsp prepared mustard
50 g/2 oz/½ cup crumbled Stilton
  cheese
4 burger buns
salt and freshly ground black pepper

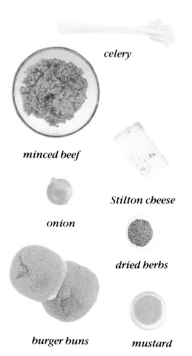

celery

minced beef

onion

Stilton cheese

dried herbs

burger buns

mustard

**1** Place the minced beef in a bowl together with the onion and celery. Season well.

**2** Stir in the herbs and mustard, bringing them together to form a firm mixture.

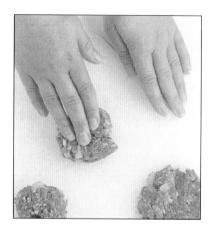

**3** Divide the mixture into eight equal portions. Place four on a chopping board and flatten each one slightly.

**4** Place the crumbled cheese in the centre of each.

**5** Flatten the remaining mixture and place on top. Mould the mixture together encasing the crumbled cheese and shape into four burgers.

**6** Grill under a medium heat for 10 minutes, turning once or until cooked through. Split the burger buns and place a burger inside each. Serve with salad and mustard pickle.

# Nachos

The addition of minced beef to this traditional starter demonstrates the use of mince as an excellent extender, creating a filling, quick meal.

## Serves 4

INGREDIENTS
225 g/8 oz/2 cups minced beef
2 red chillies, chopped
3 spring onions, chopped
175 g/6 oz nachos
300 ml/½ pint/1¼ cups soured cream
50 g/2 oz/½ cup freshly grated
  Cheddar cheese
salt and freshly ground black pepper

*chilli*

*cheese*

*minced beef*

*nachos*

*cream*

*spring onions*

**1** Dry-fry the minced beef and chillies in a large pan for 10 minutes, stirring all the time.

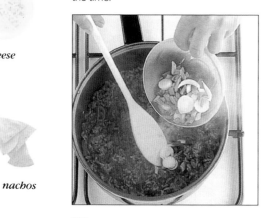

**2** Add the spring onions, season and cook for a further 5 minutes.

**3** Arrange the nachos in four individual flameproof dishes.

**4** Spoon on the minced beef mixture, top with soured cream and grated cheese. Grill under a medium heat for 5 minutes.

# Margherita

(Tomato, Basil and Mozzarella)
This classic pizza is simple to prepare. The sweet flavour of sun-ripe tomatoes works wonderfully with the basil and mozzarella.

*Serves 2–3*

INGREDIENTS
1 pizza base, about 25–30 cm/10–12 in diameter
30 ml/2 tbsp olive oil
1 quantity Tomato Sauce
150 g/5 oz mozzarella
2 ripe tomatoes, thinly sliced
6–8 fresh basil leaves
30 ml/2 tbsp freshly grated Parmesan
black pepper

*basil*

*mozzarella*

*Parmesan*

*olive oil*

*Tomato Sauce*

*tomatoes*

**1** Preheat the oven to 220°C/425°F/ Gas 7. Brush the pizza base with 15 ml/ 1 tbsp of the oil and then spread over the Tomato Sauce.

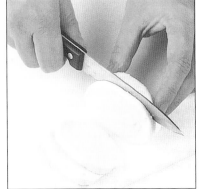

**2** Cut the mozzarella into thin slices.

**3** Arrange the sliced mozzarella and tomatoes on top of the pizza base.

**4** Roughly tear the basil leaves, add and sprinkle with the Parmesan. Drizzle over the remaining oil and season with black pepper. Bake for 15–20 minutes until crisp and golden. Serve immediately.

# Breaded Aubergine with Hot Vinaigrette

Crisp on the outside, beautifully tender within, these aubergine slices taste wonderful with a spicy dressing flavoured with chilli and capers.

COOK'S TIP
When serving a salad with a warm dressing use robust leaves that will stand up to the heat.

*Serves 2*

INGREDIENTS
1 large aubergine
50 g/2 oz/½ cup plain flour
2 eggs, beaten
115 g/4 oz/2 cups fresh
  white breadcrumbs
vegetable oil for frying
1 head radicchio
salt and freshly ground black pepper

FOR THE DRESSING
30 ml/2 tbsp olive oil
1 garlic clove, crushed
15 ml/1 tbsp capers, drained
15 ml/1 tbsp white wine vinegar
15 ml/1 tbsp chilli oil

*aubergine*

*breadcrumbs*

*eggs*

*plain flour*

*radicchio*

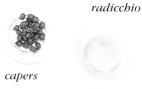

*capers*

*garlic clove*

*white wine vinegar*

**1** Top and tail the aubergine. Cut it into 5 mm/¼ in slices. Set aside.

**2** Season the flour with a generous amount of salt and black pepper. Spread out in a shallow dish. Pour the beaten eggs into a second dish, and spread out the breadcrumbs in a third.

**3** Dip the aubergine slices in the flour, then in the beaten egg and finally in the breadcrumbs, patting them on to make an even coating.

**4** Pour vegetable oil into a large frying pan to a depth of about 5 mm/¼ in. Heat the oil, then fry the aubergine slices for 3–4 minutes, turning once. Drain on kitchen paper.

**5** Heat the olive oil in a small pan. Add the garlic and the capers and cook over gentle heat for 1 minute. Increase the heat, add the vinegar and cook for 30 seconds. Stir in the chilli oil and remove the pan from the heat.

**6** Arrange the radicchio leaves on two plates. Top with the hot aubergine slices. Drizzle over the vinaigrette and serve.

# Spiced Coconut Mushrooms

Here is a simple and delicious way to cook mushrooms. They may be served with almost any Asian meal as well as with grilled or roasted meats and poultry.

*Serves 3-4*

INGREDIENTS
30 ml/2 tbsp groundnut oil
2 garlic cloves, finely chopped
2 fresh red chillies, seeded and
  sliced into rings
3 shallots, finely chopped
225 g/8 oz brown-cap
  mushrooms, thickly sliced
150 ml/¼ pint/⅔ cup coconut milk
30 ml/2 tbsp chopped fresh
  coriander
salt and ground black pepper

*red chillies*

*coconut milk*

*mushrooms*

*groundnut oil*

*coriander*

*garlic*

**1** Heat a wok until hot, add the oil and swirl it around. Add the garlic and chillies, then stir-fry for a few seconds.

**2** Add the shallots and stir-fry for 2–3 minutes until softened. Add the mushrooms and stir-fry for 3 minutes.

**3** Pour in the coconut milk and bring to the boil. Boil rapidly over a high heat until the liquid is reduced by half and coats the mushrooms. Taste and adjust the seasoning, if necessary.

**4** Sprinkle over the coriander and toss gently to mix. Serve at once.

## VARIATION
Use snipped fresh chives instead of coriander if you wish.

# Stir-fried Chickpeas

Buy canned chickpeas and you will save all the time needed for soaking and then thoroughly cooking dried chickpeas. Served with a crisp green salad, this dish makes a filling vegetarian main course for two, or could be served in smaller quantities as a starter.

*Serves 2–4 as an accompaniment*

INGREDIENTS
30 ml/2 tbsp sunflower seeds
1 × 400 g/14 oz can chickpeas, drained
5 ml/1 tsp chilli powder
5 ml/1 tsp paprika
30 ml/2 tbsp vegetable oil
1 clove garlic, crushed
200 g/7 oz canned chopped tomatoes
225 g/8 oz fresh spinach, coarse stalks removed
salt and freshly ground black pepper
10 ml/2 tsp chilli oil

*spinach*
*garlic*
*sunflower seeds*

*chickpeas*

**1** Heat the wok, and then add the sunflower seeds. Dry-fry until the seeds are golden and toasted.

**2** Remove the sunflower seeds and set aside. Toss the chickpeas in chilli powder and paprika. Remove and reserve.

**3** Heat the wok, then add the oil. When the oil is hot, stir-fry the garlic for 30 seconds, add the chickpeas and stir-fry for 1 minute.

**4** Stir in the tomatoes and stir-fry for 4 minutes. Toss in the spinach, season well and stir-fry for 1 minute. Drizzle chilli oil and scatter sunflower seeds over the vegetables, then serve.

# Asparagus Rolls with Herb Butter Sauce

For a taste sensation, try tender asparagus spears wrapped in crisp filo pastry. The buttery herb sauce makes the perfect accompaniment.

*Serves 2*

INGREDIENTS
4 sheets of filo pastry
50 g/2 oz/¼ cup butter, melted
16 young asparagus spears, trimmed

FOR THE SAUCE
2 shallots, finely chopped
1 bay leaf
150 ml/¼ pint/⅔ cup dry white wine
175 g/6 oz butter, softened
15 ml/1 tbsp chopped fresh herbs
salt and freshly ground black pepper
snipped chives, to garnish

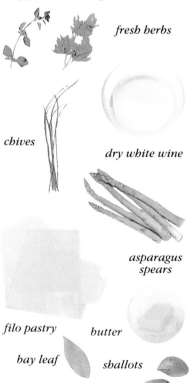

*fresh herbs*

*chives*

*dry white wine*

*asparagus spears*

*filo pastry*    *butter*

*bay leaf*    *shallots*

**1** Preheat the oven to 200°C/400°F/ Gas 6. Brush each filo sheet with melted butter. Fold one corner of the sheet down to the bottom edge to give a wedge shape.

**2** Lay 4 asparagus spears on top at the longest edge and roll up towards the shortest edge. Using the remaining filo and asparagus spears make 3 more rolls in the same way.

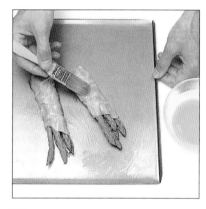

**3** Lay the rolls on a greased baking sheet. Brush with the remaining melted butter. Bake in the oven for 8 minutes until golden.

**4** Meanwhile, put the shallots, bay leaf and wine into a pan. Cover and cook over a high heat until the wine is reduced to about 45–60 ml/3–4 tbsp.

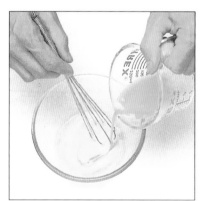

**5** Strain the wine mixture into a bowl. Whisk in the butter, a little at a time, until the sauce is smooth and glossy.

**6** Stir in the herbs and add salt and pepper to taste. Return to the pan and keep the sauce warm. Serve the rolls on individual plates with a salad garnish, if liked. Serve the butter sauce separately, sprinkled with a few snipped chives.

# Chinese Greens with Oyster Sauce

Here Chinese greens are prepared in a very simple way – stir-fried and served with oyster sauce. The combination makes a simple, quickly prepared, tasty accompaniment.

*Serves 3-4*

INGREDIENTS
450 g/1 lb Chinese greens
  (*pak choi*)
30 ml/2 tbsp groundnut oil
15–30 ml/1–2 tbsp oyster sauce

*Chinese greens*

*groundnut oil*

*oyster sauce*

## VARIATION
You can replace the Chinese greens with Chinese flowering cabbage, which is also known by its Cantonese name *choi sam*. It has bright green leaves and tiny yellow flowers, which are also eaten along with the leaves and stalks. It is available from oriental grocers.

**1** Trim the Chinese greens, removing any discoloured leaves and damaged stems. Tear into manageable pieces.

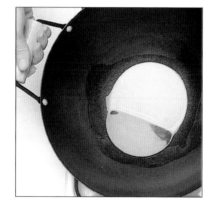

**2** Heat a wok until hot, add the oil and swirl it around.

**3** Add the Chinese greens and stir-fry for 2–3 minutes until the greens have wilted a little.

**4** Add the oyster sauce and continue to stir-fry a few seconds more until the greens are cooked but still slightly crisp. Serve immediately.

# Fish Bites with Crispy Cabbage

Add an oriental element to a special meal with these attractive and tasty fish bites. Coated in sesame seeds and served with the traditional deep-fried cabbage, they are sure to impress.

## Serves 4

INGREDIENTS
FOR THE FISH BITES
350 g/12 oz/1½ cups peeled prawns
350 g/12 oz cod fillets
10 ml/2 tsp light soy sauce
10 ml/2 tsp sesame seeds
oil for deep-frying

FOR THE CABBAGE
225 g/8 oz savoy cabbage
pinch of salt
15 g/½ oz/1 tbsp flaked almonds
spring roll sauce, to serve

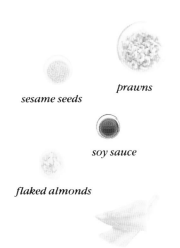

*sesame seeds*

*prawns*

*soy sauce*

*flaked almonds*

*cod fillets*

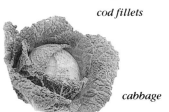

*cabbage*

**1** Put the prawns and cod in a food processor and blend for 20 seconds. Place in a bowl and stir in the soy sauce.

**2** Roll the mixture into sixteen balls and toss in the sesame seeds to coat.

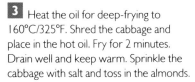

**3** Heat the oil for deep-frying to 160°C/325°F. Shred the cabbage and place in the hot oil. Fry for 2 minutes. Drain well and keep warm. Sprinkle the cabbage with salt and toss in the almonds.

**4** Fry the balls in two batches for 5 minutes until golden-brown. Remove with a draining spoon. Serve with the cabbage, and spring roll sauce for dipping.

# Deep-fried Courgettes with Chilli Sauce

Crunchy coated courgettes are great served with a fiery tomato sauce.

*Serves 2*

INGREDIENTS
15 ml/1 tbsp olive oil
1 onion, finely chopped
1 red chilli, seeded and finely diced
10 ml/2 tsp hot chilli powder
400 g/14 oz can chopped tomatoes
1 vegetable stock cube
50 ml/2 fl oz/¼ cup hot water
450 g/1 lb courgettes
150 ml/¼ pint/⅔ cup milk
50 g/2 oz/½ cup plain flour
oil for deep-frying
salt and freshly ground black pepper
thyme sprigs, to garnish

TO SERVE
lettuce leaves
watercress sprigs
slices of seeded bread

courgettes

chopped tomatoes

onion

red chilli

plain flour

stock cube

milk

chilli powder

**1** Heat the oil in a pan. Add the onion and cook for 2–3 minutes. Add the chilli. Stir in the chilli powder and cook for 30 seconds.

**2** Add the tomatoes. Crumble in the stock cube and stir in the water. Cover and cook for 10 minutes.

**3** Meanwhile, top and tail the courgettes. Cut into 5 mm/¼ in slices.

**4** Pour the milk into one shallow dish and spread out the flour in another. Dip the courgettes first in the milk, then into the flour, until well-coated.

**5** Heat the oil for deep-frying to 180°C/350°F or until a cube of bread, when added to the oil, browns in 30–45 seconds. Add the courgettes in batches and deep-fry for 3–4 minutes until crisp. Drain on kitchen paper.

**6** Place two or three lettuce leaves on each serving plate. Add a few sprigs of watercress and fan out the bread slices to one side. Season the sauce, spoon some on to each plate, top with the crisp courgettes and garnish with the thyme sprigs. Serve at once with salad and bread.

# Masala Okra

Okra, or "ladies' fingers" are a popular Indian vegetable. In this recipe they are stir-fried with a dry, spicy masala to make a delicious side dish.

### Serves 4

INGREDIENTS
450 g/1 lb okra
2.5 ml/½ tsp ground turmeric
5 ml/1 tsp chilli powder
15 ml/1 tbsp ground cumin
15 ml/1 tbsp ground coriander
1.5 ml/¼ tsp salt
1.5 ml/¼ tsp sugar
15 ml/1 tbsp lemon juice
15 ml/1 tbsp desiccated coconut
30 ml/2 tbsp chopped
    fresh coriander
45 ml/3 tbsp oil
2.5 ml/½ tsp cumin seeds
2.5 ml/½ tsp black mustard seeds
chopped fresh tomatoes, to garnish
poppadums, to serve

black mustard seeds | lemon juice | ground coriander | cumin seeds

sugar | chilli powder | ground cumin

ground turmeric | okra

desiccated coconut

salt | fresh coriander

## COOK'S TIP

When buying okra, choose firm, brightly coloured pods that are less than 10 cm/4 in long.

**1** Wash, dry and trim the okra. In a bowl, mix together the turmeric, chilli powder, cumin, ground coriander, salt, sugar, lemon juice, desiccated coconut and the fresh coriander.

**2** Heat the oil in a large frying pan. Add the cumin seeds and mustard seeds and fry for about 2 minutes, or until they begin to splutter.

**3** Add the spice mixture and continue to fry for 2 minutes.

**4** Add the okra, cover, and cook over a low heat for 10 minutes, or until tender. Garnish with chopped fresh tomatoes and serve with poppadums.

# Cannellini Bean Pureé with Grilled Radicchio

The slightly bitter flavours of the radicchio and chicory make a wonderful marriage with the creamy citrus bean purée.

*Serves 4*

INGREDIENTS
1 × 400 g/14 oz can cannellini beans
45 ml/3 tbsp low-fat fromage blanc
finely grated zest, rind and juice of 1
 large orange
15 ml/1 tbsp finely chopped fresh
 rosemary
4 heads of chicory
2 medium radicchio
15 ml/1 tbsp walnut oil

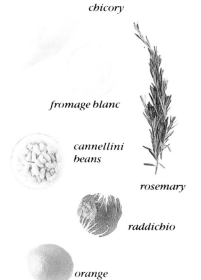

*chicory*

*fromage blanc*

*cannellini beans*

*rosemary*

*raddichio*

*orange*

**1** Drain the beans, rinse, and drain again. Purée the beans in a blender or food processor with the fromage blanc, orange zest, orange juice and rosemary. Set aside.

**2** Cut the chicory in half lengthwise.

**3** Cut each radicchio into 8 wedges.

**4** Lay out the chicory and radicchio on a baking tray and brush with walnut oil. Grill for 2–3 minutes. Serve with the puree and scatter over the orange rind.

## COOK'S TIP
Other suitable beans to use are haricot, mung or broad beans.

# Creamy Cannellini Beans with Asparagus

Cannellini beans in a creamy sauce contrast with tender asparagus in this tasty toast topper.

*Serves 2*

INGREDIENTS
10 ml/2 tsp butter
1 small onion, finely chopped
1 small carrot, grated
5 ml/1 tsp fresh thyme leaves
400 g/14 oz can cannellini
  beans, drained
150 ml/¹/₄ pint/²/₃ cup single cream
115 g/4 oz young asparagus
  spears, trimmed
2 slices of fresh cut Granary bread
salt and freshly ground black pepper

*Granary bread*  *carrot*  *thyme*

*butter*
*asparagus spears*

*single cream*

*onion*

*cannellini beans*

*parsley*

**1** Melt the butter in a pan. Add the onion and carrot and fry over a moderate heat for 4 minutes until soft. Add the thyme leaves.

**2** Rinse the cannellini beans under cold running water. Drain thoroughly, then add to the onion and carrot. Mix lightly.

**3** Pour in the cream and heat slowly to just below boiling point, stirring occasionally. Remove the pan from the heat and add salt and pepper to taste. Preheat the grill.

**4** Place the asparagus spears in a saucepan. Pour over just enough boiling water to cover. Poach for 3–4 minutes until the spears are just tender.

**5** Meanwhile, toast the bread under the grill until both sides are golden.

**6** Place the toast on individual plates. Drain the asparagus and divide the spears between the slices of toast. Spoon the bean mixture over each portion and serve.

## COOK'S TIP
Use your favourite variety of canned beans such as borlotti, haricot or flageolets.

# New Spring Salad

This chunky salad makes a satisfying meal, use other spring vegetables, if you like.

*Serves 4*

INGREDIENTS

675 g/1½ lb small new
  potatoes, halved
400 g/14 oz can broad
  beans, drained
115 g/4 oz cherry tomatoes
50 g/2 oz/2½ cups walnut halves
30 ml/2 tbsp white wine vinegar
15 ml/1 tbsp wholegrain mustard
60 ml/4 tbsp olive oil
pinch of sugar
225 g/8 oz young asparagus
  spears, trimmed
6 spring onions, trimmed
salt and freshly ground black pepper
baby spinach leaves, to serve

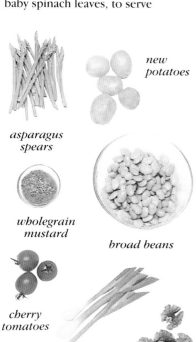

*asparagus spears*

*new potatoes*

*wholegrain mustard*

*broad beans*

*cherry tomatoes*

*spring onions*

*walnut halves*

**1** Put the potatoes in a pan. Cover with cold water and bring to the boil. Cook for 10–12 minutes, until tender. Meanwhile, tip the broad beans into a bowl. Cut the tomatoes in half and add them to the bowl with the walnuts.

**2** Put the white wine vinegar, mustard, olive oil and sugar into a jar. Add salt and pepper to taste. Close the jar tightly and shake well.

**3** Add the asparagus to the potatoes and cook for 3 minutes more. Drain the cooked vegetables well, cool under cold running water and drain again. Thickly slice the potatoes. Cut the spring onions into halves.

**4** Add the asparagus, potatoes and spring onions to the bowl containing the broad bean mixture. Pour the dressing over the salad and toss well. Serve on a bed of baby spinach leaves.

# Stir-fried Spinach with Garlic and Sesame Seeds

The sesame seeds add a crunchy texture which contrasts well with the wilted spinach in this easy vegetable dish.

*Serves 2*

INGREDIENTS
225 g/8 oz fresh spinach, washed
25 ml/1½ tbsp sesame seeds
30 ml/2 tbsp groundnut oil
1.5 ml/¼ tsp sea salt flakes
2–3 garlic cloves, sliced

*spinach*

*groundnut oil*

*garlic*

*sesame seeds*

**1** Shake the spinach to get rid of any excess water, then remove the stalks and discard any yellow or damaged leaves. Lay several spinach leaves one on top of another, roll up tightly and cut crossways into wide strips. Repeat with the remaining leaves.

**2** Heat a wok to a medium heat, add the sesame seeds and dry fry, stirring, for 1–2 minutes until golden brown. Transfer to a small bowl and set aside.

**3** Add the oil to the wok and swirl it around. When hot, add the salt, spinach and garlic and stir-fry for 2 minutes until the spinach just wilts and the leaves are coated with the oil.

**4** Sprinkle over the sesame seeds and toss well. Serve at once.

## COOK'S TIP
Take care when adding the spinach to the hot oil as it will spit furiously.

# Spring Vegetable Stir-fry

A colourful, dazzling medley of fresh and sweet young vegetables.

*Serves 4*

INGREDIENTS
15 ml/1 tbsp peanut oil
1 garlic clove, sliced
2.5 cm/1 in piece of fresh ginger root, finely chopped
115 g/4 oz baby carrots
115 g/4 oz patty pan squash
115 g/4 oz baby sweetcorn
115 g/4 oz French beans, topped and tailed
115 g/4 oz sugar-snap peas, topped and tailed
115 g/4 oz young asparagus, cut into 7.5 cm/3 in pieces
8 spring onions, trimmed and cut into 5 cm/2 in pieces
115 g/4 oz cherry tomatoes

FOR THE DRESSING
juice of 2 limes
15 ml/1 tbsp runny honey
15 ml/1 tbsp soy sauce
5 ml/1 tsp sesame oil

**1** Heat the peanut oil in a wok or large frying pan.

**2** Add the garlic and ginger and stir-fry over a high heat for 1 minute.

**3** Add the carrots, patty pan squash, sweetcorn and beans and stir-fry for another 3–4 minutes.

**4** Add the sugar-snap peas, asparagus, spring onions and cherry tomatoes and stir-fry for a further 1–2 minutes.

*spring onion*

*asparagus*

*sugar-snap peas*

*baby sweetcorn*

*lime*

*patty pan squash*

*cherry tomatoes*

*carrot*

*ginger*

*garlic*

*French beans*

**5** Mix the dressing ingredients together and add to the pan.

**6** Stir well then cover the pan. Cook for 2–3 minutes more until the vegetables are just tender but still crisp.

## COOK'S TIP
Stir-fries take only moments to cook so prepare this dish at the last minute.

# Lemon and Ginger Spicy Beans

An extremely quick delicious meal, made with canned beans for speed. You probably won't need extra salt as canned beans tend to be already salted.

*Serves 4*

### INGREDIENTS

5 cm/2 in piece fresh ginger root, peeled and roughly chopped
3 garlic cloves, roughly chopped
250 ml/8 fl oz/1 cup cold water
15 ml/1 tbsp sunflower oil
1 large onion, thinly sliced
1 fresh red chilli, seeded and finely chopped
¼ tsp cayenne pepper
10 ml/2 tsp ground cumin
5 ml/1 tsp ground coriander
½ tsp ground turmeric
30 ml/2 tbsp lemon juice
75 g/3 oz/⅓ cup chopped fresh coriander
1 × 400 g/14 oz can black-eyed beans, drained and rinsed
1 × 400 g/14 oz can aduki beans, drained and rinsed
1 × 400 g/14 oz can haricot beans, drained and rinsed
freshly ground black pepper

**1** Place the ginger, garlic and 60 ml/4 tbsp of the cold water in a blender and mix until smooth.

**2** Heat the oil in a pan. Add the onion and chilli and cook gently for 5 minutes until softened.

**3** Add the cayenne pepper, cumin, ground coriander and turmeric and stir-fry for 1 minute.

**4** Stir in the ginger and garlic paste from the blender and cook for another minute.

garlic
red chilli
aduki beans
ginger
black-eyed beans
ground coriander
ground turmeric
ground cumin
haricot beans
onion

**5** Add the remaining water, lemon juice and fresh coriander, stir well and bring to the boil. Cover the pan tightly and cook for 5 minutes.

**6** Add all the beans and cook for a further 5–10 minutes. Season with pepper and serve.

# Bengali-style Vegetables

A hot dry curry using spices that do not require long slow cooking.

## *Serves 4*

INGREDIENTS

$^{1}/_{2}$ medium cauliflower, broken into
  small florets
1 large potato, peeled and cut into
  2.5 cm/1 in dice
115 g/4 oz French beans, trimmed
2 courgettes, halved lengthways
  and sliced
2 green chillies
2.5 cm/1 in piece of fresh root
  ginger, peeled
120 ml/4 fl oz/$^{1}/_{2}$ cup natural yogurt
10 ml/2 tsp ground coriander
2.5 ml/$^{1}/_{2}$ tsp ground turmeric
25 g/1 oz/2 tbsp ghee
2.5 ml/$^{1}/_{2}$ tsp garam masala
5 ml/1 tsp cumin seeds
10 ml/2 tsp sugar
pinch each of ground cloves,
  ground cinnamon and
  ground cardamom
salt and freshly ground black pepper

**1** Bring a large pan of water to the boil. Add the cauliflower and potato and cook for 5 minutes. Add the beans and courgettes and cook for 2–3 minutes.

**2** Meanwhile, cut the chillies in half, remove the seeds and roughly chop the flesh. Finely chop the ginger. Mix the chillies and ginger in a small bowl.

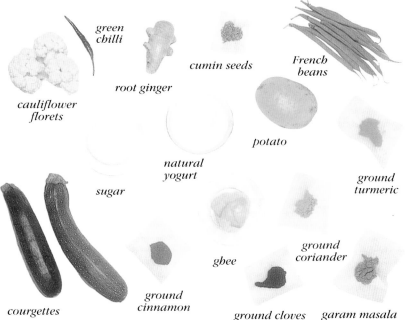

*green chilli*

*root ginger*

*cumin seeds*

*French beans*

*cauliflower florets*

*natural yogurt*

*potato*

*ground turmeric*

*sugar*

*courgettes*

*ground cinnamon*

*ghee*

*ground cloves*

*ground coriander*

*garam masala*

**3** Drain the vegetables and tip them into a bowl. Add the chilli and ginger mixture, with the yogurt, ground coriander and turmeric. Season with plenty of salt and pepper and mix well.

**4** Heat the ghee in a large frying pan. Add the vegetable mixture and cook over a high heat for 2 minutes, stirring from time to time.

**5** Stir in the garam masala and cumin seeds and cook for 2 minutes.

**6** Stir in the sugar and remaining spices and cook for 1 minute or until all the liquid has evaporated.

## COOK'S TIP

If ghee is not available you can clarify your own butter. Melt 50 g/2 oz/¼ cup butter slowly in a small pan. Remove from the heat and leave for about 5 minutes. Pour off the clear yellow clarified butter, leaving the sediment in the pan.

## Stir-fried Squid with Black Bean Sauce

If you cannot buy fresh squid you will find small or baby frozen squid, ready skinned, boned and with heads removed, at your local Oriental supermarket.

*Serves 4*

INGREDIENTS
1 large or 2 medium-sized squid
1 red chilli
10 ml/2 tsp peanut oil
1 clove garlic, crushed
30 ml/2 tbsp black bean sauce
60 ml/4 tbsp water
fresh parsley sprigs, to garnish
steamed rice, to serve

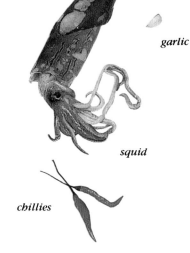

*black bean sauce*

*garlic*

*squid*

*chillies*

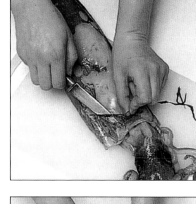

**1** Carefully remove the skin from the squid and discard.

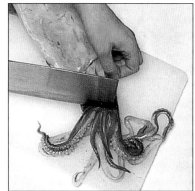

**2** Cut off the head of each squid just below the eye, and discard.

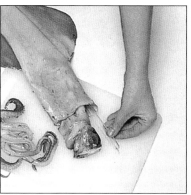

**3** Remove the bone from the squid and discard.

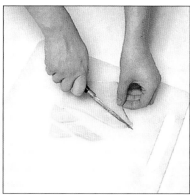

**4** Cut the squid into bite-size pieces and score the flesh in a criss-cross pattern with a sharp knife.

**5** Carefully deseed the chilli and chop it finely. Wear rubber gloves to protect your hands if necessary.

**6** Heat the wok, then add the oil. When the oil is hot, add the garlic and cook until it starts to sizzle but does not colour. Stir in the squid and fry until the flesh starts to stiffen and turn white. Quickly stir in the black bean sauce, water and chilli. Continue stirring until the squid is cooked and tender (not more than a minute). Garnish with parsley sprigs and the tentacles and serve with steamed rice.

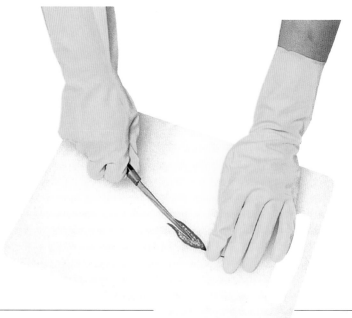

# Thai Fish Stir-fry

This is a substantial dish: it is best served with chunks of fresh crusty white bread, for mopping up all the delicious, spicy juices.

*Serves 4*

INGREDIENTS
675 g/1½ lb mixed seafood (for example, red snapper, cod, raw prawn tails) filleted and skinned
300 ml/½ pint/1¼ cups coconut milk
15 ml/1 tbsp vegetable oil
salt and freshly ground black pepper

FOR THE SAUCE
2 large red chillies
1 onion, roughly chopped
5 cm/2 in piece root ginger, peeled and sliced
5 cm/2 in piece lemon grass, outer leaf discarded, roughly sliced
5 cm/2 in piece galingale, peeled and sliced
6 blanched almonds, chopped
2.5 ml/½ tsp turmeric
2.5 ml/½ tsp salt

*chilli*

*onion*

*ginger*

*prawn*

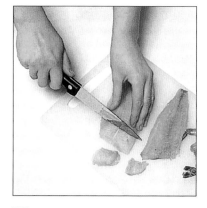

**1** Cut the filleted fish into large chunks. Peel the prawns, keeping their tails intact.

**2** Carefully remove the seeds from the chillies and chop roughly, wearing rubber gloves to protect your hands if necessary. Then, make the sauce by putting the chillies and the other sauce ingredients in the food processor with 45 ml/3 tbsp of the coconut milk. Blend until smooth.

**3** Heat the wok, then add the oil. When the oil is hot, stir-fry the seafood for 2–3 minutes, then remove.

**4** Add the sauce and the remaining coconut milk to the wok, then return the seafood. Bring to the boil, season well and serve with crusty bread.

# Cajun-style Cod

This recipe works equally well with any firm-fleshed fish such as swordfish, shark, tuna or halibut.

*Serves 4*

INGREDIENTS
4 cod steaks, each weighing about
    175 g/6 oz
30 ml/2 tbsp natural low fat yogurt
15 ml/1 tbsp lime or lemon juice
1 garlic clove, crushed
5 ml/1 tsp ground cumin
5 ml/1 tsp paprika
5 ml/1 tsp mustard powder
2.5 ml/½ tsp cayenne pepper
2.5 ml/½ tsp dried thyme
2.5 ml/½ tsp dried oregano
new potatoes and a mixed salad,
    to serve

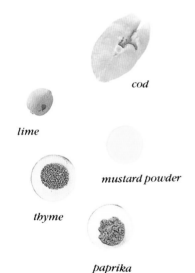

*cod*

*lime*

*mustard powder*

*thyme*

*paprika*

**1** Pat the fish dry on absorbent kitchen paper. Mix together the yogurt and lime or lemon juice and brush lightly over both sides of the fish.

**2** Mix together the garlic clove, spices and herbs. Coat both sides of the fish with the seasoning mix, rubbing in well.

## COOK'S TIP

If you don't have a ridged grill pan, heat several metal skewers under a grill until red hot. Holding the ends with a cloth, press onto the seasoned fish before cooking to give a ridged appearance.

**3** Spray a ridged grill pan or heavy-based frying pan with non-stick cooking spray. Heat until very hot. Add the fish and cook over a high heat for 4 minutes, or until the underside is well browned.

**4** Turn over and cook for a further 4 minutes, or until the steaks have cooked through. Serve immediately accompanied with new potatoes and a mixed salad.

# Pan-fried Red Mullet with Lemon

This dish, which is spectacularly attractive and delicious, is also quick and easy to make.

*Serves 4*

INGREDIENTS
1 large bulb fennel
1 lemon
12 red mullet fillets, skin left intact
45 ml/3 tbsp fresh marjoram, chopped
45 ml/3 tbsp olive oil
225 g/8 oz lamb's lettuce
salt and freshly ground black pepper

FOR THE VINAIGRETTE
200 ml/7 fl oz/generous ¾ cup
   peanut oil
15 ml/1 tbsp white wine vinegar
15 ml/1 tbsp sherry vinegar
salt and freshly ground black pepper

FOR THE SAUCE
40 g/1½ oz black olives
15 g/½ oz/1 tbsp unsalted butter
25 g/1 oz/1 tbsp capers

*fennel*

*red mullet*

*marjoram*

*lamb's lettuce*

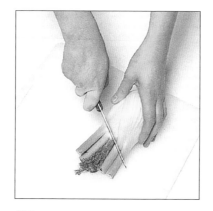

**1** Trim the fennel bulb and cut it into fine matchsticks. Peel the lemon. Remove any excess pith from the peel, then cut it into fine strips. Blanch the rind and refresh it immediately in cold water. Drain.

**2** Make the vinaigrette by placing all the ingredients in a small bowl and lightly whisking until well mixed.

**3** Sprinkle the red mullet fillets with salt, pepper and marjoram.

**4** Heat the wok and add the olive oil. When the oil is very hot, add the fennel and stir-fry for 1 minute, then drain and remove.

**5** Reheat the wok and, when the oil is hot, stir-fry the red mullet fillets, cooking them skin-side down first for 2 minutes, then flipping them over for 1 further minute. Drain well on kitchen towels and wipe the wok clean with kitchen towels.

**6** For the sauce, cut the olives into slivers. Heat the wok and add the butter. When the butter is hot, stir-fry the capers and olives for 1 minute. Toss the lamb's lettuce in the dressing. Arrange the fillets on a bed of lettuce, topped with the fennel and lemon, and serve with the olive and caper sauce.

# Jamaican Spiced Cod Steaks with Pumpkin Ragout

Spicy hot from Kingston town, this fast fish dish is guaranteed to appeal. The term 'ragout' is taken from the old French verb *ragouter*, which means to stimulate the appetite.

## Serves 4

### INGREDIENTS
finely grated zest of ½ orange
30 ml/2 tbsp black peppercorns
15 ml/1 tbsp allspice berries or
　Jamaican pepper
2.5 ml/½ tsp salt
4 × 175 g/6 oz cod steaks
groundnut oil, for frying
new potatoes, to serve (optional)
45 ml/3 tbsp chopped fresh parsley,
　to garnish

### FOR THE RAGOUT
30 ml/2 tbsp groundnut oil
1 medium onion, chopped
2.5 cm/1 in fresh root ginger, peeled
　and grated
450 g/1 lb fresh pumpkin, peeled,
　deseeded and chopped
3–4 shakes of Tabasco sauce
30 ml/2 tbsp soft brown sugar
15 ml/1 tbsp vinegar

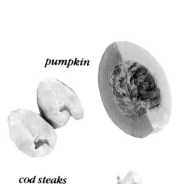

*pumpkin*

*cod steaks*

*ginger*

### COOK'S TIP
This recipe can be adapted using any type of firm pink or white fish that is available, such as haddock, whiting, monkfish, halibut or tuna.

**1** To make the ragout, heat the oil in a heavy saucepan and add the onion and ginger. Cover and cook, stirring, for 3–4 minutes until soft.

**2** Add the chopped pumpkin, Tabasco sauce, brown sugar and vinegar, cover and cook over a low heat for 10–12 minutes until softened.

**3** Combine the orange zest, peppercorns, allspice or Jamaican pepper and salt, then crush coarsely using a pestle and mortar. (Alternatively, coarsely grind the peppercorns in a pepper mill and combine with the zest and seasoning.)

**4** Scatter the spice mixture over both sides of the fish and moisten with a sprinkling of oil.

**5** Heat a large frying pan and fry the cod steaks for 12 minutes, turning once.

**6** Serve the cod steaks with a spoonful of pumpkin ragout and new potatoes, if desired, and garnish the ragout with chopped fresh parsley.

# Fish Parcels

Sea bass is good for this recipe, but you could also use small whole trout, or white fish fillet such as cod or haddock.

## Serves 4

4 pieces sea bass fillet or 4
   whole small sea bass, about
   450 g/1 lb each
oil for brushing
2 shallots, thinly sliced
1 garlic clove, chopped
15 ml/1 tbsp capers
6 sun-dried tomatoes, finely
   chopped
4 black olives, pitted and thinly
   sliced
grated rind and juice of
   1 lemon
5 ml/1 tsp paprika
salt and freshly ground black
   pepper

## COOK'S TIP
These parcels can also be baked in the oven: place them on a baking sheet and cook at 200°C/400°F/Gas Mark 6 for 15–20 minutes.

**1** Clean the fish if whole. Cut four large squares of double-thickness foil, large enough to enclose the fish; brush with a little oil.

**2** Place a piece of fish in the centre of each piece of foil and season well with salt and pepper.

**3** Scatter over the shallots, garlic, capers, tomatoes, olives and grated lemon rind. Sprinkle with the lemon juice and paprika.

*paprika*

*shallots*

*lemon*

*garlic*

*sun-dried tomatoes*

*capers*

*black olives*

*sea bass fillets*

**4** Fold the foil over to enclose the fish loosely, sealing the edges firmly so none of the juices can escape. Place on a moderately-hot barbecue and cook for 8–10 minutes. Then open up the tops of the parcels and serve.

# Spiced Scallops in their Shells

Scallops are excellent steamed. When served with this spicy sauce, they make a delicious yet simple starter. Each person spoons sauce on to the scallops before eating them.

## Serves 4

INGREDIENTS
8 scallops, shelled (ask the fishmonger to reserve the cupped side of 4 shells)
2 slices fresh root ginger, shredded
½ garlic clove, shredded
2 spring onions, green parts only, shredded
salt and pepper

FOR THE SAUCE
1 garlic clove, crushed
15 ml/1 tbsp grated fresh root ginger
2 spring onions, white parts only, chopped
1-2 fresh green chillies, seeded and finely chopped
15 ml/1 tbsp light soy sauce
15 ml/1 tbsp dark soy sauce
10 ml/2 tsp sesame oil

scallops

spring onions

ginger

garlic

light soy sauce

dark soy sauce

green chilli

sesame oil

**1** Remove the dark beard-like fringe and tough muscle from the scallops.

**2** Place 2 scallops in each shell. Season lightly with salt and pepper, then scatter the ginger, garlic and spring onions on top. Place the shells in a bamboo steamer and steam for about 6 minutes until the scallops look opaque (you may have to do this in batches).

**3** Meanwhile, mix together all the sauce ingredients and pour into a small serving bowl.

**4** Carefully remove each shell from the steamer, taking care not to spill the juices, and arrange them on a serving plate with the sauce bowl in the centre. Serve at once.

# Spiced Prawns with Coconut

This spicy dish is based on *Sambal Goreng Udang*, which is Indonesian in origin. It is best served with plain boiled rice.

### Serves 3-4

INGREDIENTS

2-3 fresh red chillies, seeded and chopped
3 shallots, chopped
1 lemon grass stalk, chopped
2 garlic cloves, chopped
thin sliver of dried shrimp paste
2.5 ml/½ tsp ground galangal
5 ml/1 tsp ground turmeric
5 ml/1 tsp ground coriander
15 ml/1 tbsp groundnut oil
250 ml/8 fl oz/1 cup water
2 fresh kaffir lime leaves
5 ml/1 tsp light brown soft sugar
2 tomatoes, peeled, seeded and chopped
250 ml/8 fl oz/1 cup coconut milk
675 g/1½ lb large raw prawns, peeled and deveined
squeeze of lemon juice
salt, to taste
shredded spring onions and flaked coconut, to garnish

*turmeric*

*prawns*

*red chillies*

*garlic*

*lemon grass*

*dried shrimp paste*

*coriander*

*galangal*

*groundnut oil*

*coconut milk*

*sugar*

*tomatoes*

*shallots*

*kaffir lime leaves*

**1** In a mortar pound the chillies, shallots, lemon grass, garlic, shrimp paste, galangal, turmeric and coriander with a pestle until it forms a paste.

### COOK'S TIP
Dried shrimp paste, much used in South-east Asia, is available from oriental stores.

**2** Heat a wok until hot, add the oil and swirl it around. Add the spiced paste and stir-fry for about 2 minutes. Pour in the water and add the kaffir lime leaves, sugar and tomatoes. Simmer for 8–10 minutes until most of the liquid has evaporated.

**3** Add the coconut milk and prawns and cook gently, stirring, for about 4 minutes until the prawns are pink. Taste and adjust the seasoning with salt and a squeeze of lemon juice. Serve at once, garnished with shredded spring onions and toasted flaked coconut.

# Red Snapper with Ginger and Spring Onions

This is a classic Chinese way of cooking fish. To partially cook and enhance the flavour of the spring onions and ginger, slowly pour hot oil over them.

*Serves 2-3*

INGREDIENTS
1 red snapper, about
   675-900 g/1½-2 lb, cleaned and
   scaled with head left on
1 bunch spring onions, cut into
   thin shreds
2.5 cm/1 in piece fresh root
   ginger, cut into thin shreds
1.5 ml/¼ tsp salt
1.5 ml/¼ tsp caster sugar
45 ml/3 tbsp groundnut oil
5 ml/1 tsp sesame oil
30-45 ml/2-3 tbsp light soy sauce
spring onion brushes, to garnish

*spring onions*

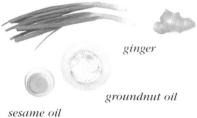

*ginger*

*sesame oil*

*groundnut oil*

*red snapper*

*light soy sauce*

*caster sugar*

### COOK'S TIP
If the fish is too big to fit inside the steamer, cut off the head and place it alongside the body – it can then be reassembled after it is cooked for serving.

**1** Rinse the fish, then pat dry with kitchen paper. Slash the flesh diagonally, three times on each side. Set the fish on a heatproof oval plate that will fit inside your bamboo steamer.

**2** Tuck about one-third of the spring onions and ginger inside the body cavity. Place the plate inside the steamer, cover with its lid, then place in a wok.

**3** Steam over a medium heat for 10–15 minutes until the fish flakes easily when tested with the tip of a knife.

**4** Carefully remove the plate from the steamer. Sprinkle over the salt, sugar and remaining spring onions and ginger.

**5** Heat the oils in a small pan until very hot, then slowly pour over the fish.

**6** Drizzle over the soy sauce and serve at once, garnished with spring onion brushes.

# Smoked Haddock Fillets with Quick Parsley Sauce

Make any herb sauce with this method, making sure it is thickened and seasoned well to complement the smoky flavour of the fish.

*Serves 4*

INGREDIENTS
4 × 225 g/8 oz smoked haddock fillets
75 g/3 oz/6 tbsp butter, softened
25 g/1 oz/2 tbsp plain flour
300 ml/½ pint/1¼ cups milk
salt and freshly ground black pepper
60 ml/4 tbsp chopped fresh parsley

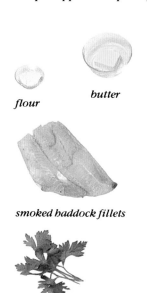

*flour*

*butter*

*smoked haddock fillets*

*parsley*

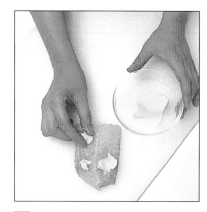

**1** Smear the fish fillets on both sides with 50 g/2 oz/4 tbsp butter and pre-heat the grill.

**2** Beat the remaining butter and flour together to make a thick paste.

**3** Grill the fish for 10–15 minutes turning when necessary. Meanwhile, heat the milk until just below boiling point. Add the flour mixture in small knobs whisking constantly over the heat. Continue until the sauce is smooth and thick.

**4** Stir in the seasoning and parsley and serve poured over the fillets.

# Thick Cod Fillet with Fresh Mixed-herb Crust

Mixed fresh herbs make this a delicious crust. Season well and serve with large lemon wedges.

*Serves 4*

INGREDIENTS

25 g/1 oz/2 tbsp butter
15 ml/1 tbsp fresh chervil
15 ml/1 tbsp fresh parsley
15 ml/1 tbsp fresh chives
175 g/6 oz/3 cups wholemeal breadcrumbs
4 × 225 g/8 oz thickly cut cod fillets, skinned
15 ml/1 tbsp olive oil
lemon wedges, to garnish
salt and freshly ground black pepper

*butter*

*breadcrumbs*

*parsley*

*cod fillets*

*chervil*

*lemon*

**1** Pre-heat the oven to 200°C/400°F/Gas 6. Melt the butter and chop the herbs finely.

**2** Mix the butter with the breadcrumbs, herbs and seasoning.

**3** Press a quarter of the mixture on top of each fillet. Place on a baking sheet and drizzle over the olive oil. Bake in the pre-heated oven for 15 minutes until the fish flesh is firm and the top turns golden. Serve garnished with lemon wedges.

# Fillets of Pink Trout with Tarragon Cream Sauce

If you do not like the idea of cooking and serving trout on the bone, ask your fishmonger to fillet and skin the fish. Serve two fillets per person.

*Serves 4*

INGREDIENTS
25 g/1 oz/2 tbsp butter
4 fresh trout, filleted and skinned
salt and freshly ground black pepper
new potatoes, to serve
runner beans, to serve

FOR THE CREAM SAUCE
2 large spring onions, white part
   only, chopped
½ cucumber, peeled, deseeded and
   cut into short batons
5 ml/1 tsp cornflour
150 ml/¼ pint/⅔ cup single cream
50 ml/2 fl oz/¼ cup dry sherry
30 ml/2 tbsp chopped fresh tarragon
1 tomato, chopped and deseeded

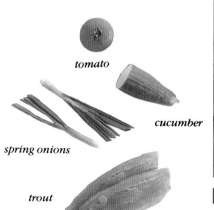

tomato

cucumber

spring onions

trout

cream

tarragon

## VARIATION

This recipe can also be made with salmon fillets and the dry sherry may be substituted with white wine.

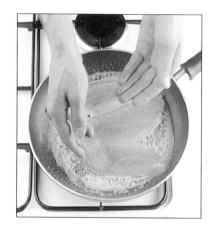

**1** Melt the butter in a large frying pan, season the fillets and cook for 6 minutes, turning once. Transfer to a plate, cover and keep warm.

**2** To make the sauce, add the spring onions and cucumber to the pan, and cook over a gentle heat, stirring, until soft but not coloured.

**3** Remove the pan from the heat and stir in the cornflour.

**4** Return to the heat and pour in the cream and sherry. Simmer to thicken, stirring continuously.

**5** Add the chopped tarragon and tomato, and season to taste.

**6** Spoon the sauce over the fillets and serve with buttered new potatoes and runner beans.

# Sizzling Beef with Celeriac Straw

The crisp celeriac matchsticks look like fine pieces of straw when cooked and have a mild celery-like flavour that is quite delicious.

*Serves 4*

INGREDIENTS
450 g/1 lb celeriac
150 ml/¼ pint/⅔ cup vegetable oil
1 red pepper
6 spring onions
450 g/1 lb rump steak
60 ml/4 tbsp beef stock
30 ml/2 tbsp sherry vinegar
10 ml/2 tsp Worcestershire sauce
10 ml/2 tsp tomato purée
salt and freshly ground black pepper

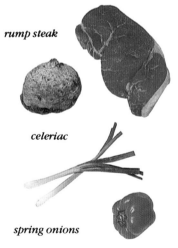

*rump steak*

*celeriac*

*spring onions*

*pepper*

**1** Peel the celeriac and then cut it into fine matchsticks, using a cleaver.

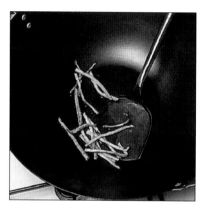

**2** Heat the wok, then add two-thirds of the oil. When the oil is hot, fry the celeriac matchsticks in batches until golden brown and crispy. Drain well on kitchen towels.

**3** Chop the red pepper and the spring onions into 2.5 cm/1 in lengths, using diagonal cuts.

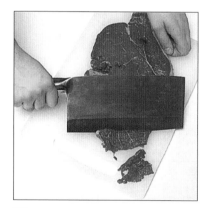

**4** Chop the beef into strips, across the grain of the meat.

**5** Heat the wok, and then add the remaining oil. When the oil is hot, stir-fry the chopped spring onions and red pepper for 2–3 minutes.

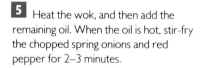

**6** Add the beef strips and stir-fry for a further 3–4 minutes until well browned. Add the stock, vinegar, Worcestershire sauce and tomato purée. Season well and serve with the celeriac straw.

# Spicy Beef

Promoting a fast-growing trend in worldwide cuisine, the wok is used in this recipe to produce a colourful and healthy meal.

*Serves 4*

INGREDIENTS
15 ml/1 tbsp oil
450 g/1 lb/4 cups minced beef
2.5 cm/1 in fresh root ginger, sliced
5 ml/1 tsp Chinese five-spice powder
1 red chilli, sliced
50 g/2 oz mangetout
1 red pepper, seeded and chopped
1 carrot, sliced
115 g/4 oz beansprouts
15 ml/1 tbsp sesame oil

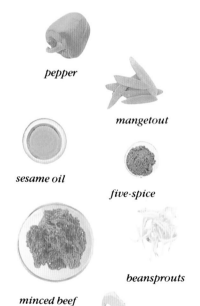

*pepper*

*mangetout*

*sesame oil*

*five-spice*

*beansprouts*

*minced beef*

*ginger*

*carrot*

*chilli*

**1** Heat the oil in a wok until almost smoking. Add the minced beef and cook for 3 minutes, stirring all the time.

**2** Add the ginger, Chinese five-spice powder and chilli. Cook for 1 minute.

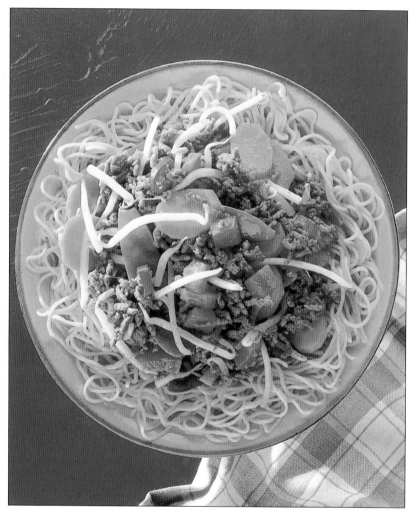

**3** Add the mangetout, pepper and carrot and cook for a further 3 minutes, stirring continuously.

**4** Add the beansprouts and sesame oil and cook for a final 2 minutes. Serve immediately with noodles.

# Glazed Lamb

Lemon and honey make a classically good combination in sweet dishes, and this lamb recipe shows how well they work together in savoury dishes, too. Serve with a fresh mixed salad to complete this delicious dish.

## Serves 4

INGREDIENTS

450 g/1 lb boneless lean lamb
15 ml/1 tbsp grapeseed oil
175 g/6 oz mangetout peas, topped
   and tailed
3 spring onions, sliced
30 ml/2 tbsp clear honey
juice of half a lemon
30 ml/2 tbsp fresh coriander, chopped
15 ml/1 tbsp sesame seeds
salt and freshly ground black pepper

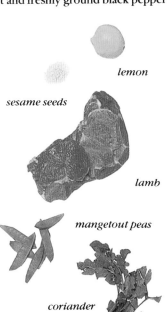

lemon

sesame seeds

lamb

mangetout peas

coriander

**1** Using a sharp knife, cut the lamb into thin strips.

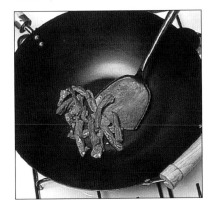

**2** Heat the wok, then add the oil. When the oil is hot, stir-fry the lamb until browned all over. Remove from the wok and keep warm.

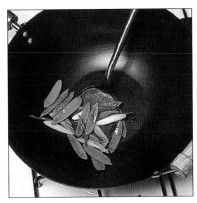

**3** Add the mangetout peas and spring onions to the hot wok and stir-fry for 30 seconds.

**4** Return the lamb to the wok and add the honey, lemon juice, coriander and sesame seeds, and season well. Bring to the boil and bubble for 1 minute until the lamb is well coated in the honey mixture.

# Sukiyaki-style Beef

This Japanese dish is a meal in itself; the recipe incorporates all the traditional elements – meat, vegetables, noodles and beancurd. If you want to do it all properly, eat the meal with chopsticks, and a spoon to collect the stock juices.

*Serves 4*

INGREDIENTS
450 g/1 lb thick rump steak
200 g/7 oz Japanese rice noodles
15 ml/1 tbsp shredded suet
200 g/7 oz hard beancurd, cut
   into cubes
8 shitake mushrooms, trimmed
2 medium leeks, sliced into 2.5 cm/
   1 in lengths
90 g/3½ oz baby spinach, to serve

FOR THE STOCK
15 ml/1 tbsp caster sugar
90 ml/6 tbsp rice wine
45 ml/3 tbsp dark soy sauce
125 ml/4 fl oz/½ cup water

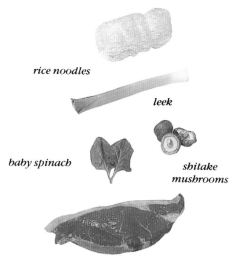

*rice noodles*

*leek*

*baby spinach*

*shitake mushrooms*

*rump steak*

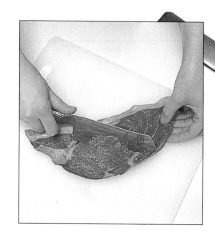

**1** Cut the beef into thin slices.

**2** Blanch the noodles in boiling water for 2 minutes. Strain well.

**3** Mix together all the stock ingredients in a bowl.

**4** Heat the wok, then add the suet. When the suet is melted, stir-fry the beef for 2–3 minutes until it is cooked, but still pink in colour.

**5** Pour the stock over the beef.

**6** Add the remaining ingredients and cook for 4 minutes, until the leeks are tender. Serve a selection of the different ingredients, with a few baby spinach leaves, to each person.

# Veal Escalopes with Artichokes

Artichokes are very hard to prepare fresh, so use canned artichoke hearts, instead – they have an excellent flavour and are simple to use.

*Serves 4*

INGREDIENTS
450 g/1 lb veal escalopes
1 shallot
115 g/4 oz smoked bacon,
  finely chopped
1 × 400 g/14 oz can of artichoke
  hearts in brine, drained and
  quartered
150 ml/¼ pint/⅔ cup veal stock
3 fresh rosemary sprigs
60 ml/4 tbsp double cream
salt and freshly ground black pepper
fresh rosemary sprigs, to garnish

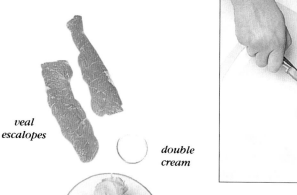

*veal escalopes*

*double cream*

*artichoke hearts*

**1** Cut the veal into thin slices.

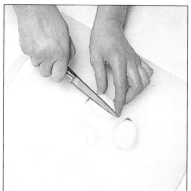

**2** Using a sharp knife, cut the shallot into thin slices.

**3** Heat the wok, then add the bacon. Stir-fry for 2 minutes. When the fat is released, add the veal and shallot and stir-fry for 3–4 minutes.

**4** Add the artichokes and stir-fry for 1 minute. Stir in the stock and rosemary and simmer for 2 minutes. Stir in the double cream, season with salt and pepper and serve garnished with sprigs of fresh rosemary.

# Chicken Liver Kebabs

These may be barbecued outdoors and served with salads and baked potatoes or grilled indoors and served with rice and broccoli.

*Serves 4*

INGREDIENTS

115 g/4 oz rindless streaky bacon rashers
350 g/12 oz chicken livers
12 large (no need to pre-soak) stoned prunes
12 cherry tomatoes
8 button mushrooms
30 ml/2 tbsp olive oil

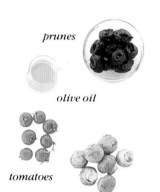

*prunes*

*olive oil*

*tomatoes*

*mushrooms*

*bacon*

*chicken livers*

**1** Cut each rasher of bacon into two pieces, wrap a piece around each chicken liver and secure in position with wooden cocktail sticks.

**2** Wrap the stoned prunes around the cherry tomatoes.

**3** Thread the bacon-wrapped livers onto metal skewers with the tomatoes and prunes. Brush with oil. Cover the tomatoes and prunes with a strip of foil to protect them while grilling or barbecuing. Cook for 5 minutes on each side.

**4** Remove the cocktail sticks and serve the kebabs immediately.

# Pan-fried Pork with Peaches and Green Peppercorns

**When peaches are in season, consider this speedy pork dish, brought alive with green peppercorns.**

*Serves 4*

INGREDIENTS
400 g/14 oz/2 cups long-grain rice
1 litre/1¾ pints/4 cups chicken stock
4 × 200 g/7 oz pork chops or
   loin pieces
30 ml/2 tbsp vegetable oil
30 ml/2 tbsp dark rum or sherry
1 small onion, chopped
3 large ripe peaches
15 ml/1 tbsp green peppercorns
15 ml/1 tbsp white wine vinegar
salt and freshly ground black pepper

*onion*

*pork chops*

*dark rum*

*oil*

*green peppercorns*

*white wine vinegar*

*peaches*

## VARIATION
If peaches are not ripe when picked, they can be difficult to peel. Only tree ripened fruit is suitable for peeling. If fresh peaches are out of season, a can of sliced peaches may be used instead.

**1** Cover the rice with 900 ml/1½ pints/ 3¾ cups chicken stock. Stir, bring to a simmer and cook uncovered for 15 minutes. Switch off the heat and cover for 5 minutes. Season the pork with a generous twist of black pepper. Heat a large bare metal frying pan and moisten the pork with 15 ml/1 tbsp of the oil. Cook for 12 minutes, turning once.

**2** Transfer the meat to a warm plate. Pour off the excess fat from the pan and return to the heat. Allow the sediment to sizzle and brown, add the rum or sherry and loosen the sediment with a flat wooden spoon. Pour the pan contents over the meat, cover and keep warm. Wipe the pan clean.

**3** Heat the remaining vegetable oil in the pan and soften the onion over a steady heat.

**4** Cover the peaches with boiling water to loosen the skins, then peel, slice and discard the stones.

**5** Add the peaches and peppercorns to the onion and coat for 3–4 minutes, until they begin to soften.

**6** Add the remaining chicken stock and simmer briefly. Return the pork and meat juices to the pan, sharpen with vinegar, and season to taste. Serve with the rice.

# Wild Mushroom Rösti with Bacon and Eggs

Dried ceps or porcini mushrooms, commonly found in Italian delicatessens, are a good substitute for fresh. Cook them in a potato rösti and serve with bacon and a fried egg for breakfast or a lazy supper.

*Serves 4*

INGREDIENTS
675 g/1½ lb floury potatoes, peeled
10 g/¼ oz dried ceps or porcini
  mushrooms
2 fresh thyme sprigs, chopped
30 ml/2 tbsp chopped fresh parsley
60 ml/4 tbsp vegetable oil, for frying
4 × 115 g/4 oz gammon or
  unsmoked bacon
pinch of salt
4 eggs, to serve
1 bunch watercress, to serve

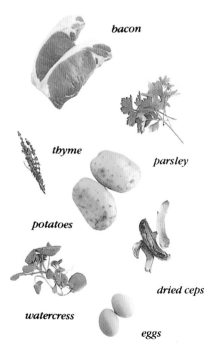

*bacon*

*thyme*

*parsley*

*potatoes*

*dried ceps*

*watercress*

*eggs*

## COOK'S TIP

A large rösti can be made in a non-stick frying pan. Allow 12 minutes to cook. Half-way through the cooking time, invert the rösti on a large plate and slide back into the pan.

**1** Bring the potatoes to the boil in a large saucepan of salted water and cook for 5 minutes.

**2** Cover the mushrooms with boiling water to soften, then chop roughly.

**3** Drain the potatoes, allow them to cool and grate them coarsely. Add the mushrooms, thyme and parsley and combine together well.

**4** Heat 30 ml/2 tbsp of the oil in a frying pan, spoon in the rösti mixture in heaps and flatten. Fry for 6 minutes, turning once during cooking.

**5** Preheat a moderate grill and cook the gammon or bacon slices until they sizzle at the edges.

**6** Heat the remaining oil in a frying pan and fry the eggs as you like them. Serve the rösti together with the eggs and bacon and a watercress salad.

# Stir-fried Pork with Mustard

Fry the apples for this dish very carefully, because they will disintegrate if they are overcooked.

*Serves 4*

INGREDIENTS

500 g/1¼ lb pork fillet
1 tart apple, such as Granny Smith
40 g/1½ oz/3 tbsp unsalted butter
15 ml/1 tbsp caster sugar
1 small onion, finely chopped
30 ml/2 tbsp Calvados or
    other brandy
15 ml/1 tbsp Meaux or coarse-grain
    mustard
150 ml/¼ pint/⅔ cup double cream
30 ml/2 tbsp fresh parsley, chopped
salt and freshly ground black pepper
flat-leaf parsley sprigs, to garnish

*pork fillet*

*onion*

*mustard*

*apple*

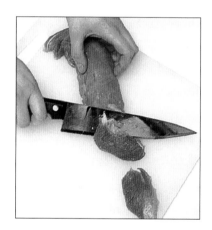

**1** Cut the pork fillet into thin slices.

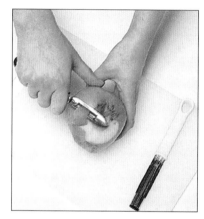

**2** Peel and core the apple. Cut it into thick slices.

**3** Heat the wok, then add half the butter. When the butter is hot, add the apple slices, sprinkle over the sugar, and stir-fry for 2–3 minutes. Remove the apple and set aside. Wipe out the wok with kitchen towels.

**4** Heat the wok, then add the remaining butter and stir-fry the pork fillet and onion together for 2–3 minutes, until the pork is golden and the onion has begun to soften.

**5** Stir in the Calvados or other brandy and boil until it is reduced by half. Stir in the mustard.

**6** Add the cream and simmer for about 1 minute, then stir in the parsley. Serve garnished with sprigs of flat-leaf parsley.

# Chinese Duck in Pitta

This recipe is based on Chinese crispy duck but uses duck breast instead of whole duck. After 15 minutes' cooking, the duck breast will still have a pinkish tinge. If you like it well cooked, leave it in the oven for a further 5 minutes.

## *Makes 2*

**INGREDIENTS**
1 duck breast, weighing about 175 g/
    6 oz
3 spring onions
7.5 cm/3 in piece cucumber
2 round pitta breads
30 ml/2 tbsp hoi-sin sauce
radish chrysanthemum and spring
    onion tassel, to garnish

*pitta breads*

*cucumber*

*duck breast*

*hoi-sin sauce*

*spring onions (scallions)*

**1** Preheat the oven to 220°C/425°F/gas mark 7. Skin the duck breast, place the skin and breast separately on a rack and cook in the oven for 10 minutes.

**2** Remove the skin from the oven, cut into pieces and return to the oven for a further 5 minutes.

**3** Meanwhile, cut the spring onions and cucumber piece into fine shreds about 4 cm/1½ in long.

**4** Heat the pitta bread in the oven for a few minutes until puffed up, then split in half to make a pocket.

**5** Slice the duck breast thinly.

**6** Stuff the duck breast into the pitta bread with a little spring onion, cucumber, crispy duck skin and some hoi-sin sauce. Serve garnished with a radish chrysanthemum and spring onion tassel.

# Stir-fried Turkey with Broccoli and Mushrooms

This is a really easy, tasty supper dish which works well with chicken too.

*Serves 4*

INGREDIENTS
115 g/4 oz broccoli florets
4 spring onions
5 ml/1 tsp cornflour
45 ml/3 tbsp oyster sauce
15 ml/1 tbsp dark soy sauce
120 ml/4 fl oz/½ cup
  chicken stock
10 ml/2 tsp lemon juice
45 ml/3 tbsp groundnut oil
450 g/1 lb turkey steaks, cut into
  strips, about 5 mm x 5 cm/
  ¼ x 2 in
1 small onion, chopped
2 garlic cloves, crushed
10 ml/2 tsp grated fresh
  root ginger
115 g/4 oz fresh shiitake
  mushrooms, sliced
75 g/3 oz baby sweetcorn,
  halved lengthways
15 ml/1 tbsp sesame oil
salt and ground black pepper
egg noodles, to serve

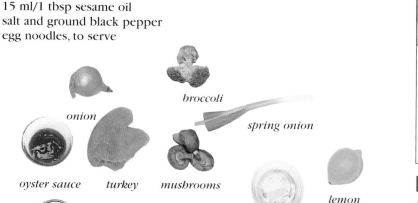

*onion*

*broccoli*

*spring onion*

*oyster sauce*  *turkey*  *mushrooms*

*lemon*

*dark soy sauce*

*groundnut oil*

*baby sweetcorn*

*garlic*

*chicken stock*

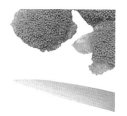

**1** Divide the broccoli florets into smaller sprigs and cut the stalks into thin diagonal slices.

**2** Finely chop the white parts of the spring onions and slice the green parts into thin shreds.

**3** In a bowl, blend together the cornflour, oyster sauce, soy sauce, stock and lemon juice. Set aside.

**4** Heat a wok until hot, add 30 ml/ 2 tbsp of the groundnut oil and swirl it around. Add the turkey and stir-fry for about 2 minutes until golden and crispy at the edges. Remove the turkey from the wok and keep warm.

**5** Add the remaining groundnut oil to the wok and stir-fry the chopped onion, garlic and ginger over a medium heat for about 1 minute. Increase the heat to high, add the broccoli, mushrooms and sweetcorn and stir-fry for 2 minutes.

**6** Return the turkey to the wok, then add the sauce with the chopped spring onion and seasoning. Cook, stirring, for about 1 minute until the sauce has thickened. Stir in the sesame oil. Serve immediately on a bed of egg noodles with the finely shredded spring onion scattered on top.

# Chicken Liver Stir-fry

The final sprinkling of lemon, parsley and garlic gives this dish a delightful fresh flavour and wonderful aroma.

### Serves 4

INGREDIENTS

500 g/1¼ lb chicken livers
75 g/3 oz/6 tbsp butter
175 g/6 oz field mushrooms
50 g/2 oz chanterelle mushrooms
3 cloves garlic, finely chopped
2 shallots, finely chopped
150 ml/¼ pint/⅔ cup medium sherry
3 fresh rosemary sprigs
30 ml/2 tbsp fresh parsley, chopped
rind of 1 lemon, grated
salt and freshly ground pepper
fresh rosemary sprigs, to garnish
4 thick slices of white toast, to serve

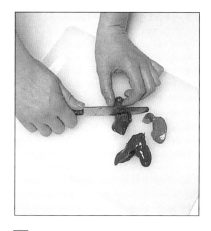

**1** Clean and trim the chicken livers to remove any gristle or muscle.

**2** Season the livers generously with salt and freshly ground black pepper, tossing well to coat thoroughly.

*chanterelle mushrooms*

*field mushroom*

*lemon*

*rosemary*

**3** Heat the wok and add 15 g/½ oz/ 1 tbsp of the butter. When melted, add the livers in batches (melting more butter where necessary but reserving 25 g/1 oz/ 2 tbsp for the vegetables) and flash-fry until golden brown. Drain with a slotted spoon and transfer to a plate, then place in a low oven to keep warm.

**4** Cut the field mushrooms into thick slices and, depending on the size of the chanterelles, cut in half.

**5** Heat the wok and add the remaining butter. When melted, stir in two-thirds of the chopped garlic and the shallots and stir-fry for 1 minute until golden brown. Stir in the mushrooms and continue to cook for a further 2 minutes.

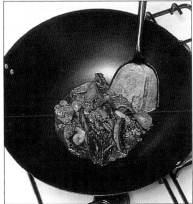

**6** Add the sherry, bring to the boil and simmer for 2–3 minutes until syrupy. Add the rosemary, salt and pepper and return livers to the pan. Stir-fry for 1 minute. Garnish with extra sprigs of rosemary, and serve sprinkled with a mixture of lemon, parsley and the remaining chopped garlic, with slices of toast.

# Indonesian-style Satay Chicken

Use boneless chicken thighs to give a good flavour to these satays.

*Serves 4*

INGREDIENTS

50 g/2 oz/½ cup raw peanuts
45 ml/3 tbsp vegetable oil
1 small onion, finely chopped
2.5 cm/1 in piece root ginger, peeled and finely chopped
1 clove garlic, crushed
675 g/1½ lb chicken thighs, skinned and cut into cubes
90 g/3½ oz creamed coconut, roughly chopped
15 ml/1 tbsp chilli sauce
60 ml/4 tbsp crunchy peanut butter
5 ml/1 tsp soft dark brown sugar
150 ml/¼ pint/⅔ cup milk
1.2 ml/¼ tsp salt

**1** Shell and rub the skins from the peanuts, then soak them in enough water to cover, for 1 minute. Drain the nuts and cut them into slivers.

**2** Heat the wok and add 5 ml/1 tsp oil. When the oil is hot, stir-fry the peanuts for 1 minute until crisp and golden. Remove with a slotted spoon and drain on kitchen towels.

**3** Add the remaining oil to the hot wok. When the oil is hot, add the onion, ginger and garlic and stir-fry for 2–3 minutes until softened but not browned. Remove with a slotted spoon and drain on kitchen towels.

*creamed coconut*

*peanuts*

*chilli sauce*

*peanut butter*

**4** Add the chicken pieces and stir-fry for 3–4 minutes until crisp and golden on all sides. Thread on to pre-soaked bamboo skewers and keep warm.

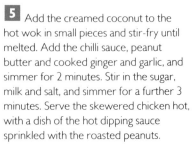

**5** Add the creamed coconut to the hot wok in small pieces and stir-fry until melted. Add the chilli sauce, peanut butter and cooked ginger and garlic, and simmer for 2 minutes. Stir in the sugar, milk and salt, and simmer for a further 3 minutes. Serve the skewered chicken hot, with a dish of the hot dipping sauce sprinkled with the roasted peanuts.

# Glazed Chicken with Cashew Nuts

Hoisin sauce lends a sweet yet slightly hot note to this chicken dish, while cashew nuts add a pleasing contrast of texture.

*Serves 4*

INGREDIENTS
75 g/3 oz/¾ cup cashew nuts
1 red pepper
450 g/1 lb skinless and boneless
    chicken breasts
45 ml/3 tbsp groundnut oil
4 garlic cloves, finely chopped
30 ml/2 tbsp Chinese rice wine
    or medium-dry sherry
45 ml/3 tbsp hoisin sauce
10 ml/2 tsp sesame oil
5–6 spring onions, green parts
    only, cut into
        2.5 cm/1 in lengths

*chicken*

*spring onion*

*red pepper*

*cashew nuts*

*Chinese rice wine*

*garlic*

*groundnut oil*

*hoisin sauce*

*sesame oil*

VARIATION
Use blanched almonds instead of cashew nuts if you prefer.

**1** Heat a wok until hot, add the cashew nuts and stir-fry over a low to medium heat for 1–2 minutes until golden brown. Remove and set aside.

**2** Halve the pepper and remove the seeds. Slice the pepper and chicken into finger-length strips.

**3** Heat the wok again until hot, add the oil and swirl it around. Add the garlic and let it sizzle in the oil for a few seconds. Add the pepper and chicken and stir-fry for 2 minutes.

**4** Add the rice wine or sherry and hoisin sauce. Continue to stir-fry until the chicken is tender and all the ingredients are evenly glazed.

**5** Stir in the sesame oil, toasted cashew nuts and spring onion tips. Serve immediately with rice or noodles.

## Caesar Salad

There are many stories about the origin of Caesar Salad. The most likely is that it was invented by an Italian, Caesar Cardini, who owned a restaurant in Mexico in the 1920s. Simplicity is the key to its success.

*Serves 4*

INGREDIENTS
3 slices day-old bread, 1 cm/½ in
  thick
60 ml/4 tbsp garlic oil
salt and pepper
50 g/2 oz piece Parmesan cheese
1 cos lettuce

DRESSING
2 egg yolks, as fesh as possible
25 g/1 oz canned anchovy fillets,
  roughly chopped
½ tsp French mustard
120 ml/½ fl oz/½ cup olive oil,
  preferably Italian
15 ml/1 tbsp white wine vinegar

### COOK'S TIP

The classic dressing for Caesar Salad is made with raw egg yolks. Ensure you use only the freshest eggs, bought from a reputable dealer. Expectant mothers, young children and the elderly are not advised to eat raw egg yolks. You could omit them from the dressing and grate hard-boiled yolks on top of the salad instead.

**1** To make the dressing, combine the egg yolks, anchovies, mustard, oil and vinegar in a screw-top jar and shake well.

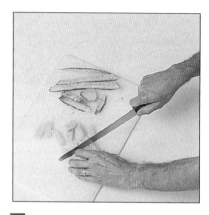

**2** Remove the crusts from the bread with a serrated knife and cut into 2.5 cm/ 1 in fingers.

**3** Heat the garlic oil in a large frying pan (skillet), add the pieces of bread and fry until golden. Sprinkle with salt and leave to drain on absorbent kitchen paper.

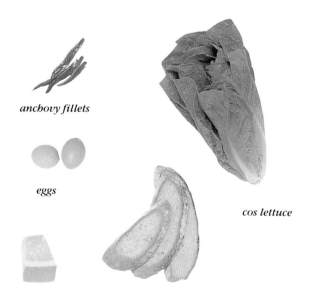

*anchovy fillets*

*eggs*

*cos lettuce*

*Parmesan cheese*       *bread*

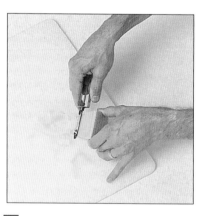

**4** Cut thin shavings from the Parmesan cheese with a vegetable peeler.

**5** Wash the salad leaves and spin dry. Smother with the dressing, and scatter with garlic croûtons and Parmesan cheese. Season and serve.

# Rocket, Pear and Parmesan Salad

For a sophisticated start to an elaborate meal, try this simple salad of honey-rich pears, fresh Parmesan and aromatic leaves of rocket. Enjoy with a young Beaujolais or chilled Lambrusco wine.

*Serves 4*

INGREDIENTS
3 ripe pears, Williams or Packhams
10 ml/2 tsp lemon juice
45 ml/3 tbsp hazelnut or walnut oil
115 g/4 oz rocket
75 g/3 oz Parmesan cheese
black pepper
open-textured bread, to serve

*rocket*

*Parmesan cheese*

*pears*

**1** Peel and core the pears and slice thickly. Moisten with lemon juice to keep the flesh white.

**2** Combine the nut oil with the pears. Add the rocket leaves and toss.

**3** Turn the salad out on to 4 small plates and top with shavings of Parmesan cheese. Season with freshly ground black pepper and serve.

## COOK'S TIP
If you are unable to buy rocket easily, you can grow your own from early spring to late summer.

# Melon and Parma Ham Salad with Strawberry Salsa

Sections of cool fragrant melon wrapped with slices of air-dried ham make a delicious salad starter. If strawberries are in season, serve with a savoury-sweet strawberry salsa and watch it disappear.

*Serves 4*

INGREDIENTS
1 large melon, cantaloupe, galia or charentais
175 g/6 oz Parma or Serrano ham, thinly sliced

FOR THE SALSA
225 g/8 oz strawberries
5 ml/1 tsp caster sugar
30 ml/2 tbsp groundnut or sunflower oil
15 ml/1 tbsp orange juice
½ tsp finely grated orange zest
½ tsp finely grated fresh root ginger
salt and ground black pepper

**2** To make the salsa, hull the strawberries and cut them into large dice. Place in a small mixing bowl with the sugar and crush lightly to release the juices. Add the oil, orange juice, zest and ginger. Season with salt and a generous twist of black pepper.

**3** Arrange the melon on a serving plate, lay the ham over the top and serve with a bowl of salsa.

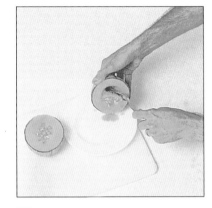

**1** Halve the melon and take the seeds out with a spoon. Cut the rind away with a paring knife, then slice the melon thickly. Chill until ready to serve.

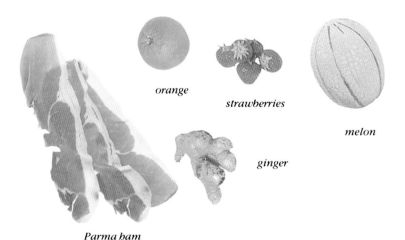

*orange*

*strawberries*

*melon*

*ginger*

*Parma ham*

# Chicken Liver Salad

This salad may be served as a first course on individual plates.

*Serves 4*

INGREDIENTS
mixed salad leaves, e.g. frisée and
    oakleaf lettuce or radicchio
1 avocado, diced
2 pink grapefruits, segmented
350 g/12 oz chicken livers
30 ml/2 tbsp olive oil
1 garlic clove, crushed
salt and freshly ground black pepper
crusty bread, to serve

FOR THE DRESSING
30 ml/2 tbsp lemon juice
60 ml/4 tbsp olive oil
2.5 ml/½ tsp wholegrain mustard
2.5 ml/½ tsp clear honey
15 ml/1 tbsp snipped fresh chives

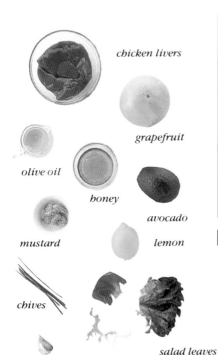

chicken livers

grapefruit

olive oil

honey

avocado

mustard          lemon

chives

salad leaves

garlic

**1** First prepare the dressing: put all the ingredients into a screw-topped jar and shake vigorously to emulsify. Taste and adjust the seasoning.

**2** Wash and dry the salad. Arrange attractively on a serving plate with the avocado and grapefruit.

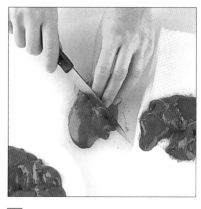

**3** Dry the chicken livers on paper towels and remove any unwanted pieces. Cut the larger livers in half and leave the smaller ones whole.

**4** Heat the oil in a large frying pan. Stir-fry the livers and garlic briskly until the livers are brown all over (they should be slightly pink inside).

**5** Season with salt and freshly ground black pepper and drain on paper towels.

**6** Place the liver on the salad and spoon over the dressing. Serve immediately with warm crusty bread.

# Fresh Spinach and Avocado Salad

Young tender spinach leaves make a change from lettuce and are delicious served with avocado, cherry tomatoes and radishes in a tofu sauce.

*Serves 2-3*

INGREDIENTS
1 large avocado
juice of 1 lime
225 g/8 oz fresh baby spinach leaves
115 g/4 oz cherry tomatoes
4 spring onions, sliced
1/2 cucumber
50 g/2 oz radishes, sliced

FOR THE DRESSING
115 g/4 oz soft silken tofu
45 ml/3 tbsp milk
10 ml/2 tsp mustard
2.5 ml/1/2 tsp white wine vinegar
pinch of cayenne
salt and freshly ground black pepper

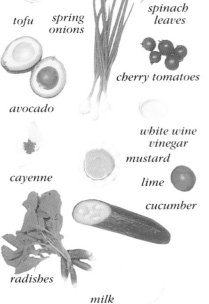

*tofu*   *spring onions*   *spinach leaves*

*cherry tomatoes*

*avocado*

*white wine vinegar*
*mustard*

*cayenne*   *lime*

*cucumber*

*radishes*

*milk*

**1** Cut the avocado in half, remove the stone and strip off the skin. Cut the flesh into slices. Transfer to a plate, drizzle over the lime juice and set aside.

**2** Wash and dry the spinach leaves. Put them in a mixing bowl.

## COOK'S TIP
Use soft silken tofu rather than the firm block variety. It can be found in most supermarkets in long-life cartons.

**3** Cut the larger cherry tomatoes in half and add all the tomatoes to the mixing bowl, with the spring onions. Cut the cucumber into chunks and add to the bowl with the sliced radishes.

**4** Make the dressing. Put the tofu, milk, mustard, wine vinegar and cayenne in a food processor or blender. Add salt and pepper to taste. Process for 30 seconds until smooth. Scrape the dressing into a bowl and add a little extra milk if you like a thinner dressing. Sprinkle with a little extra cayenne and garnish with radish roses and herb sprigs, if liked.

# Roquefort and Walnut Pasta Salad

This is a simple earthy salad, relying totally on the quality of the ingredients. There is no real substitute for the Roquefort – a blue-veined ewe's-milk cheese from south-western France.

*Serves 4*

INGREDIENTS
225 g/8 oz/2 cups pasta shapes
selection of salad leaves such as
  rocket, curly endive, lamb's lettuce
baby spinach or radicchio)
30 ml/2 tbsp walnut oil
60 ml/4 tbsp sunflower oil
30 ml/2 tbsp red wine vinegar or
  sherry vinegar
salt and ground black pepper
225 g/8 oz Roquefort cheese,
  roughly crumbled
115 g/4 oz/1 cup walnut halves

*pasta shapes*

*Roquefort cheese*     *walnuts*

*salad leaves*

## COOK'S TIP
Try toasting the walnuts under the grill for a couple of minutes to release the flavour.

**1** Cook the pasta in plenty of boiling salted water according to the manufacturer's instructions. Drain well and cool. Wash and dry the salad leaves and place in a bowl.

**2** Whisk together the walnut oil, sunflower oil, vinegar and salt and pepper to taste.

**3** Pile the pasta in the centre of the leaves, scatter over the crumbled Roquefort and pour over the dressing.

**4** Scatter over the walnuts. Toss just before serving.

# Prawn and Mint Salad

Green prawns make all the difference to this salad, as the flavours marinate well into the prawns before cooking. Garnish with shavings of fresh coconut for a tropical topping.

## Serves 4

INGREDIENTS
12 large green prawns
15 ml/1 tbsp unsalted butter
15 ml/1 tbsp fish sauce
juice of 1 lime
45 ml/3 tbsp thin coconut milk
5 ml/1 tsp caster sugar
1 garlic clove, crushed
2.5 cm/1 in piece of root ginger, peeled and grated
2 fresh red chillies, seeded and finely chopped
freshly ground black pepper
30 ml/2 tbsp fresh mint leaves
225 g/8 oz light green lettuce leaves, to serve

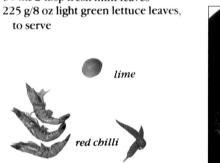

lime

red chilli

prawns

fish sauce

coconut milk

mint

ginger

 lettuce

**1** Peel the prawns leaving the tails intact.

**2** Remove the vein.

**3** Melt the butter in a large frying pan and toss in the green prawns until they turn pink.

**4** Mix the fish sauce, lime juice, coconut milk, sugar, garlic, ginger, chillies and pepper together.

**5** Toss the warm prawns into the sauce with the mint leaves. Serve the prawn mixture on a bed of green lettuce leaves.

## VARIATION
The prawns can be substituted with lobster tails if you are feeling extravagant.

# Tomato and Feta Cheese Salad

Sweet sun-ripened tomatoes are rarely more delicious than when served with feta cheese and olive oil. This salad, popular in Greece and Turkey, is enjoyed as a light meal with pieces of crispy bread.

### Serves 4

INGREDIENTS
900 g/2 lb tomatoes
200 g/7 oz feta cheese
125 ml/4 fl oz/½ cup olive oil,
   preferably Greek
12 black olives
4 sprigs fresh basil
black pepper

## COOK'S TIP
Feta cheese has a strong flavour and can be salty. The least salty variety is imported from Greece and Turkey, and is available from specialist delicatessens.

**2** Slice the tomatoes thickly and arrange in a shallow dish.

**3** Crumble the cheese over the tomatoes, sprinkle with olive oil, then strew with olives and fresh basil. Season with freshly ground black pepper and serve at room temperature.

**1** Remove the tough cores from the tomatoes with a small knife.

tomatoes

basil

feta cheese

olives

# Tuna Fish and Flageolet Bean Salad

Two cans of tuna fish form the basis of this delicious store cupboard salad.

## Serves 4

**INGREDIENTS**

90 ml/6 tbsp mayonnaise
5 ml/1 tsp mustard
30 ml/2 tbsp capers
45 ml/3 tbsp chopped fresh parsley
pinch of celery salt
2 × 200 g/7 oz cans tuna fish in oil, drained
3 little gem lettuces
1 × 400 g/14 oz can flageolet beans, drained
1 × 400 g/14 oz can baby artichoke hearts, halved
12 cherry tomatoes, halved
toasted sesame bread, to serve

**1** Combine the mayonnaise, mustard, capers and parsley in a mixing bowl. Season to taste with celery salt. Flake the tuna into the dressing and toss gently.

**2** Arrange the lettuce leaves on four plates, then spoon the tuna mixture onto the leaves.

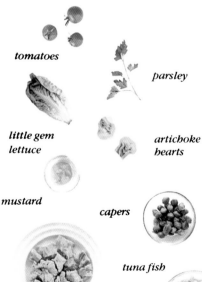

*tomatoes*

*parsley*

*little gem lettuce*

*artichoke hearts*

*mustard*

*capers*

*tuna fish*

*flageolet beans*

**3** Spoon the flageolet beans to one side, followed by the tomatoes and artichoke hearts. Serve with slices of toasted sesame bread.

## VARIATION

Flageolet beans are taken from the under-developed pods of haricot beans. They have a sweet creamy flavour and an attractive green colour. If not available, use white haricot or cannellini beans.

# Courgette Puffs with Salad and Balsamic Dressing

This unusual salad consists of deep-fried courgettes, flavoured with mint and served warm on a bed of salad leaves with a balsamic dressing.

*Serves 2*

INGREDIENTS
450 g/1 lb courgettes
75 g/3 oz/1½ cups fresh white
  breadcrumbs
1 egg
pinch of cayenne pepper
15 ml/1 tbsp chopped fresh mint
oil for deep-frying
15 ml/1 tbsp/3 tbsp balsamic vinegar
45 ml/3 tbsp extra virgin olive oil
200 g/7 oz mixed salad leaves
salt and freshly ground black pepper

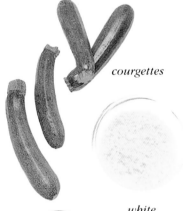
*courgettes*

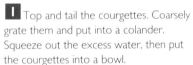
*white breadcrumbs*

*balsamic vinegar*

*mixed salad leaves*

*egg*

*mint*

**1** Top and tail the courgettes. Coarsely grate them and put into a colander. Squeeze out the excess water, then put the courgettes into a bowl.

**2** Add the breadcrumbs, egg, cayenne, mint and seasoning. Mix well.

**3** Shape the courgette mixture into balls, about the size of walnuts.

**4** Heat the oil for deep-frying to 180°C/350°F or until a cube of bread, when added to the oil, browns in 30–40 seconds. Deep-fry the courgette balls in batches for 2–3 minutes. Drain on kitchen paper.

**5** Whisk the vinegar and oil together and season well.

**6** Put the salad leaves in a bowl and pour over the dressing. Add the courgette puffs and toss lightly together. Serve at once, while the courgette puffs are still crisp.

# Chicory, Fruit and Nut Salad

Mildly bitter chicory is wonderful with sweet fruit, and is especially delicious when complemented by a creamy curry sauce.

## Serves 4

INGREDIENTS
45 ml/3 tbsp mayonnaise
15 ml/1 tbsp Greek yogurt
15 ml/1 tbsp mild curry paste
90 ml/6 tbsp single cream
$^1/_2$ iceberg lettuce
2 heads of chicory
50 g/2 oz/$^1/_2$ cup cashew nuts
50 g/2 oz/$1^1/_4$ cups flaked coconut
2 red apples
75 g/3 oz/$^1/_2$ cup currants

*iceberg lettuce*

*currants*

*curry paste*  *mayonnaise*

*cashew nuts*  *red apples*

*single cream*

*flaked coconut*

*chicory*

**1** Mix the mayonnaise, Greek yogurt, curry paste and single cream in a small bowl. Cover and chill until required.

**2** Tear the iceberg lettuce into pieces and put into a mixing bowl.

**3** Cut the root end off each head of chicory, separate the leaves and add them to the lettuce. Preheat the grill.

**4** Toast the cashew nuts for 2 minutes until golden. Tip into a bowl and set aside. Spread out the coconut flakes on a baking sheet. Grill for 1 minute until golden.

**5** Quarter the apples and cut out the cores. Slice the apples and add to the lettuce with the coconut, cashew nuts and currants.

## COOK'S TIP
Watch the coconut and cashew nuts very carefully when grilling, as they brown very fast.

**6** Spoon the dressing over the salad, toss lightly and serve.

# Chicken and Pasta Salad

This is a delicious way to use up left-over cooked chicken, and makes a filling meal.

*Serves 4*

INGREDIENTS

225 g/8 oz tri-coloured
  pasta twists
30 ml/2 tbsp bottled pesto sauce
15 ml/1 tbsp olive oil
1 beefsteak tomato
12 stoned black olives
225 g/8 oz cooked French beans
350 g/12 oz cooked chicken, cubed
salt and freshly ground black pepper
fresh basil, to garnish

tomato

pesto sauce

French beans

basil

olive oil

pasta twists

chicken

black olives

**1** Cook the pasta in plenty of boiling, salted water until *al dente* (about 12 minutes or as directed on the packet).

**2** Drain the pasta and rinse in plenty of cold running water. Put into a bowl and stir in the pesto sauce and olive oil.

**3** Skin the tomato by placing in boiling water for about 10 seconds and then into cold water, to loosen the skin.

**4** Cut the tomato into small cubes and add to the pasta with the olives, seasoning and French beans cut into 4 cm/1 ½ in lengths. Add the cubed chicken. Toss gently together and transfer to a serving platter. Garnish with fresh basil.

# Poor Boy Steak Salad

'Poor Boy' started life in the Italian Creole community of New Orleans when the poor survived on sandwiches filled with left-over scraps. Times have improved since then, and today the 'Poor Boy' sandwich is commonly filled with tender beef steak and other goodies. This is a salad version of 'Poor Boy'.

### Serves 4

**INGREDIENTS**

4 sirloin or rump steaks, each
   weighing 175 g/6 oz
1 escarole lettuce
1 bunch watercress
4 tomatoes, quartered
4 large gherkins, sliced
4 spring onions, sliced
4 canned artichoke hearts, halved
175 g/6 oz button mushrooms, sliced
12 green olives
125 ml/4fl oz French dressing
salt and ground black pepper

**1** Season the steaks with black pepper. Cook the steaks under a moderate grill for 6–8 minutes, turning once, until medium-rare. Cover and leave to rest in a warm place.

*steaks*

*gherkins (dill pickles)*

*artichoke hearts*

*spring onions*

*watercress*

*mushrooms*

*olives*

*tomatoes*

**2** Wash the salad leaves and spin dry. Combine with the remainder of the ingredients (except the steak) and toss with the French Dressing.

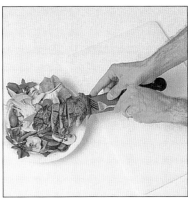

**3** Divide the salad between 4 plates. Slice each steak diagonally and position over the salad. Season with salt and serve.

# Avocado, Tomato and Mozzarella Pasta Salad with Pine Nuts

A salad made from ingredients representing the colours of the Italian flag – a sunny cheerful dish!

*Serves 4*

### INGREDIENTS
175 g/6 oz/1½ cups pasta bows
6 ripe red tomatoes
225 g/8 oz mozzarella cheese
1 large ripe avocado
30 ml/2 tbsp pine nuts, toasted
1 sprig fresh basil, to garnish

### DRESSING
90 ml/6 tbsp olive oil
30 ml/2 tbsp wine vinegar
5 ml/1 tsp balsamic vinegar (optional)
5 ml/1 tsp wholegrain mustard
pinch of sugar
salt and pepper
30 ml/2 tbsp chopped fresh basil

*olive oil*

*avocado*

*tomatoes*

*mozzarella cheese*

*basil*

*pine nuts*    *pasta bows*

**1** Cook the pasta in plenty of boiling salted water according to the manufacturer's instructions. Drain well and cool.

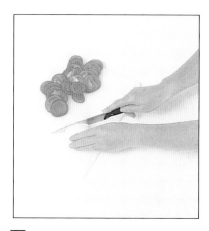

**2** Slice the tomatoes and mozzarella cheese into thin rounds.

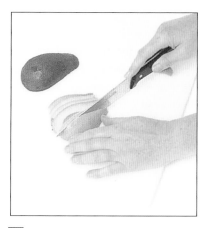

**3** Halve the avocado, remove the stone and gently peel off the skin. Slice the flesh lengthways.

**4** Whisk all the dressing ingredients together in a small bowl.

**5** Arrange the tomato, mozzarella and avocado in overlapping slices around the edge of a flat plate.

**6** Toss the pasta with half the dressing and the chopped basil. Pile into the centre of the plate. Pour over the remaining dressing, scatter over the pine nuts and garnish with a sprig of fresh basil. Serve immediately.

# Thai Seafood Salad

This seafood salad with chilli, lemon grass and fish sauce is light and refreshing.

## Serves 4

INGREDIENTS
225 g/8 oz ready-prepared squid
225 g/8 oz raw tiger prawns
8 scallops, shelled
225 g/8 oz firm white fish
30–45 ml/2–3 tbsp olive oil
small mixed lettuce leaves and
   coriander sprigs, to serve

FOR THE DRESSING
2 small fresh red chillies, seeded
   and finely chopped
5 cm/2 in piece lemon grass,
   finely chopped
2 fresh kaffir lime leaves,
   shredded
30 ml/2 tbsp Thai fish sauce
   (*nam pla*)
2 shallots, thinly sliced
30 ml/2 tbsp lime juice
30 ml/2 tbsp rice vinegar
10 ml/2 tsp caster sugar

*white fish*          *squid*

*scallops*

*tiger prawns*

*lemon grass*

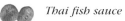

*Thai fish sauce*

*shallots*          *kaffir lime leaves*

**1** Prepare the seafood: slit open the squid bodies, score the flesh with a sharp knife, then cut into square pieces. Halve the tentacles, if necessary. Peel and devein the prawns. Remove the dark beard-like fringe and tough muscle from the scallops. Cube the white fish.

**2** Heat a wok until hot. Add the oil and swirl it around, then add the prawns and stir-fry for 2–3 minutes until pink. Transfer to a large bowl. Stir-fry the squid and scallops for 1–2 minutes until opaque. Remove and add to the prawns. Stir-fry the white fish for 2–3 minutes. Remove and add to the cooked seafood. Reserve any juices.

**3** Put all the dressing ingredients in a small bowl with the reserved juices from the wok; mix well.

**4** Pour the dressing over the seafood and toss gently. Arrange the salad leaves and coriander sprigs on four individual plates, then spoon the seafood on top. Serve at once.

# Wholemeal Pasta, Asparagus and Potato Salad with Parmesan

**A meal in itself, this is a real treat when made with fresh asparagus just in season.**

*Serves 4*

INGREDIENTS
225 g/8 oz/2 cups wholemeal
    pasta shapes
60 ml/4 tbsp extra virgin olive oil
salt and ground black pepper
350 g/12 oz baby new potatoes
225 g/8 oz fresh asparagus
115 g/4 oz piece fresh
    Parmesan cheese

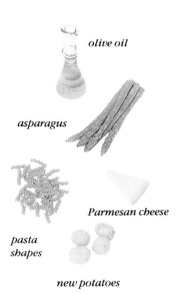

*olive oil*

*asparagus*

*Parmesan cheese*

*pasta shapes*

*new potatoes*

**1** Cook the pasta in boiling salted water according to the manufacturer's instructions. Drain well and toss with the olive oil, salt and pepper while still warm.

**2** Wash the potatoes and cook in boiling salted water for 12–15 minutes or until tender. Drain and toss with the pasta.

**3** Trim any woody ends off the asparagus and halve the stalks if very long. Blanch in boiling salted water for 6 minutes until bright green and still crunchy. Drain. Plunge into cold water to stop them cooking and allow to cool. Drain and dry on kitchen paper.

**4** Toss the asparagus with the potatoes and pasta, season and transfer to a shallow bowl. Using a rotary vegetable peeler, shave the Parmesan over the salad.

# Mediterranean Salad with Basil

A type of Salade Niçoise with pasta, conjuring up all the sunny flavours of the Mediterranean.

## Serves 4

### INGREDIENTS
225 g/8 oz/2 cups chunky pasta shapes
175 g/6 oz fine green beans
2 large ripe tomatoes
50 g/2 oz fresh basil leaves
200 g/7 oz can tuna fish in oil, drained
2 hard-boiled eggs, shelled and sliced
   or quartered
50 g/2 oz can anchovy fillets, drained
capers and black olives

### DRESSING
90 ml/6 tbsp extra-virgin olive oil
30 ml/2 tbsp white wine vinegar or
   lemon juice
2 garlic cloves, crushed
2.5 ml/½ tsp Dijon mustard
30 ml/2 tbsp chopped fresh basil
salt and pepper

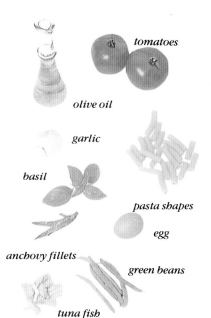

*tomatoes*

*olive oil*

*garlic*

*basil*

*pasta shapes*

*egg*

*anchovy fillets*

*green beans*

*tuna fish*

**1** Whisk all the ingredients for the dressing together and leave to infuse while you make the salad.

**2** Cook the pasta in plenty of boiling salted water according to the manufacturer's instructions. Drain well and cool.

**3** Trim the beans and blanch in boiling salted water for 3 minutes. Drain and refresh in cold water.

**4** Slice or quarter the tomatoes and arrange on the bottom of a bowl. Moisten with a little dressing and cover with a quarter of the basil leaves. Then cover with the beans. Moisten with a little more dressing and cover with a third of the remaining basil.

**5** Cover with the pasta tossed in a little more dressing, half the remaining basil and the roughly flaked tuna.

**6** Arrange the eggs on top, then finally scatter over the anchovy fillets, capers and black olives. Pour over the remaining dressing and garnish with the remaining basil. Serve immediately. Don't be tempted to chill this salad – all the flavour will be dulled.

# Grilled Pepper Salad

Grilled peppers are delicious served hot with a
sharp dressing. You can also serve them cold.

## Serves 2

INGREDIENTS
1 red pepper
1 green pepper
1 yellow or orange pepper
$^1/_2$ radicchio, separated into leaves
$^1/_2$ frisée, separated into leaves
7.5 ml/1$^1/_2$ tsp white wine vinegar
30 ml/2 tbsp extra virgin olive oil
175 g/6 oz goat's cheese
salt and freshly ground black pepper

*frisée*

*red pepper*

*green pepper*

*goat's cheese*

*yellow pepper*

*white wine vinegar*

*radicchio*

**1** Preheat the grill. Cut all the peppers in half. Cut each half into pieces.

**2** Put the pepper pieces on a rack set over a grill pan. Grill for 10 minutes.

**3** Meanwhile, divide the radicchio and frisée leaves between two plates. Chill until required.

**4** Mix the vinegar and olive oil in a jar. Add salt and pepper to taste, close the jar tightly and shake well.

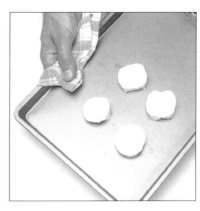

**5** Slice the goat's cheese, place on a baking sheet and grill for 1 minute.

**6** Arrange the peppers and grilled goat's cheese on the salads. Pour over the dressing and grind a little extra black pepper over each.

## COOK'S TIP
Grill the peppers until they just start to blacken around the edges – don't let them burn.

# Parmesan and Poached Egg Salad with Croûtons

Soft poached eggs, hot garlic croûtons and cool, crisp salad leaves make an unforgettable combination.

## Serves 2

INGREDIENTS

¹/₂ small loaf white bread
75 ml/5 tbsp extra virgin olive oil
2 eggs
115 g/4 oz mixed salad leaves
2 garlic cloves, crushed
7.5 ml/¹/₂ tbsp white wine vinegar
25 g/1 oz Parmesan cheese

*Parmesan cheese*

*mixed salad leaves*    *white bread*

*garlic cloves*    *eggs*

**1** Remove the crust from the bread. Cut the bread into 2.5 cm/1 in cubes.

**2** Heat 30 ml/2 tbsp of the oil in a frying pan. Cook the bread for about 5 minutes, tossing the cubes occasionally, until they are golden brown.

**3** Meanwhile, bring a pan of water to the boil. Carefully slide in the eggs, one at a time. Gently poach the eggs for 4 minutes until lightly cooked.

**5** Heat the remaining oil in the pan, add the garlic and vinegar and cook over high heat for 1 minute. Pour the warm dressing over each salad.

**4** Divide the salad leaves between two plates. Remove the croûtons from the pan and arrange them over the leaves. Wipe the pan clean with kitchen paper.

## COOK'S TIP
Add a dash of vinegar to the water before poaching the eggs. This helps to keep the whites together. To ensure that a poached egg has a good shape, swirl the water with a spoon, whirlpool-fashion, before sliding in the egg.

**6** Place a poached egg on each salad. Scatter with shavings of Parmesan and a little freshly ground black pepper, if liked.

# Penne with Spinach

### Serves 4

INGREDIENTS

225 g/8 oz fresh spinach
1 garlic clove, crushed
1 shallot or small onion,
    finely chopped
½ small red pepper, seeded and
    finely chopped
1 small red chilli, seeded
    and chopped
150 ml/¼ pint/⅔ cup stock
350 g/12 oz penne
150 g/5 oz smoked turkey rashers
45 ml/3 tbsp low-fat crème fraîche
30 ml/2 tbsp grated
    Parmesan cheese
shavings of Parmesan cheese,
    to garnish

*red pepper*

*grated Parmesan cheese*

*red chilli*

*shallot*

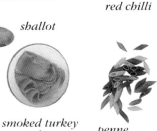

*smoked turkey rashers*

*penne*

*stock*

*low-fat crème fraîche*

*garlic*

*spinach*

**2** Put the garlic, shallot or small onion, pepper and chilli into a large frying pan. Add the stock, cover and cook for about 5 minutes until tender. Add the prepared spinach and cook quickly for a further 2–3 minutes until it has wilted.

**1** Wash the spinach and remove the hard central stalks. Shred finely.

**3** Cook the pasta in a large pan of boiling, salted water until *al dente*. Drain thoroughly.

**4** Grill the smoked turkey rashers, cool a little, and chop finely.

**5** Stir the crème fraîche and grated Parmesan into the pasta with the spinach, and toss carefully together.

**6** Transfer to serving plates and sprinkle with chopped turkey and shavings of Parmesan cheese.

# Green Pasta with Avocado Sauce

This is an unusual sauce with a pale green colour, studded with red tomato. It has a luxurious velvety texture. The sauce is rather rich, so you don't need too much of it.

*Serves 6*

INGREDIENTS
3 ripe tomatoes
2 large ripe avocados
25 g/1 oz/2 tbsp butter, plus extra for
    tossing the pasta
1 garlic clove, crushed
450 ml/12 fl oz/1½ cups
    double cream
salt and ground black pepper
dash of Tabasco sauce
450 g/1b green tagliatelle
freshly grated Parmesan cheese
60 ml/4 tbsp soured cream

*tagliatelle*

*tomatoes*

*avocado*

*garlic*

**1** Halve the tomatoes and remove the cores. Squeeze out the seeds and cut the tomatoes into dice. Set aside.

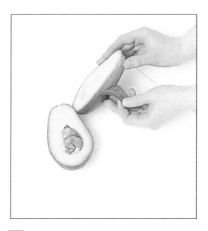

**2** Halve the avocados, take out the stones and peel. Roughly chop up the flesh.

**3** Melt the butter in a saucepan and add the garlic. Cook for 1 minute, then add the cream and chopped avocados. Raise the heat, stirring constantly to break up the avocados.

**4** Add the diced tomatoes and season to taste with salt, pepper and a little Tabasco sauce. Keep warm.

**5** Cook the pasta in plenty of boiling salted water according to the manufacturer's instructions. Drain well and toss with a knob of butter.

**6** Divide the pasta between 4 warmed bowls and spoon over the sauce. Sprinkle with grated Parmesan and top with a spoonful of soured cream.

# Pasta with Prawns and Feta Cheese

This dish combines the richness of fresh prawns with the tartness of feta cheese. Goat's cheese could also be used.

*Serves 4*

INGREDIENTS

450 g/1 lb medium raw prawns
6 spring onions
50 g/2 oz/4 tbsp butter
225 g/8 oz feta cheese
small bunch fresh chives
450 g/1 lb/4 cups penne, garganelle or rigatoni
salt and ground black pepper

*penne*

*spring onions*

*feta*

*chives*

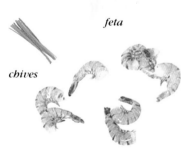

*prawns*

**1** Remove the heads from the prawns by twisting and pulling off. Peel the prawns and discard the shells. Chop the spring onions.

**2** Melt the butter in a frying pan and stir in the prawns. When they turn pink, add the spring onions and cook gently for 1 minute.

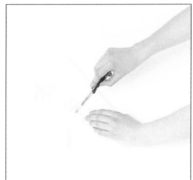

**3** Cut the feta into 1 cm/½ in cubes.

**4** Stir the feta cheese into the prawn mixture and season with black pepper.

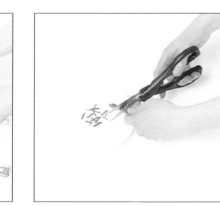

**5** Cut the chives into 2.5 cm/1 in lengths and stir half into the prawns.

**6** Cook the pasta in plenty of boiling salted water according to the manufacturer's instructions. Drain well, pile into a warmed serving dish and top with the sauce. Scatter with the remaining chives and serve.

# Mushroom Bolognese

A quick – and exceedingly tasty – vegetarian version of the classic Italian meat dish.

*Serves 4*

INGREDIENTS
450 g/1 lb mushrooms
15 ml/1 tbsp olive oil
1 onion, chopped
1 garlic clove, crushed
15 ml/1 tbsp tomato purée
400 g/14 oz can chopped tomatoes
15 ml/1 tbsp chopped fresh oregano
450 g/1 lb fresh pasta
Parmesan cheese, to serve
chopped fresh oregano, to garnish

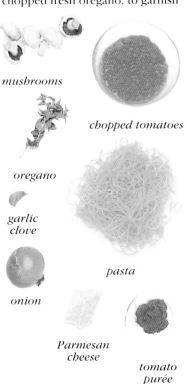

*mushrooms*

*chopped tomatoes*

*oregano*

*garlic clove*

*pasta*

*onion*

*Parmesan cheese*

*tomato purée*

**1** Trim the mushroom stems neatly, then cut each mushroom into quarters.

**2** Heat the oil in a large pan. Add the chopped onion and garlic and cook for 2–3 minutes.

**3** Add the mushrooms to the pan and cook over a high heat for 3–4 minutes, stirring occasionally.

**4** Stir in the tomato purée, chopped tomatoes and oregano. Lower the heat, cover and cook for 5 minutes.

**5** Meanwhile, bring a large pan of salted water to the boil. Cook the pasta for 2–3 minutes until just tender.

## COOK'S TIP

If you prefer to use dried pasta, make this the first thing that you cook. It will take 10–12 minutes, during which time you can make the mushroom mixture. Use 350 g/12 oz dried pasta.

**6** Season the bolognese sauce with salt and pepper. Drain the pasta, tip it into a bowl and add the mushroom mixture. Toss to mix. Serve in individual bowls, topped with shavings of fresh Parmesan cheese and a sprinkling of chopped fresh oregano.

# Fettuccine all'Alfredo

A classic dish from Rome, Fettuccine all'Alfredo is simply pasta tossed with double cream, butter and freshly grated Parmesan cheese. Popular additions are peas and strips of ham.

*Serves 4*

INGREDIENTS
25 g/1 oz/2 tbsp butter
150 ml/5 fl oz/⅔ cup double
   cream, plus 60 ml/4 tbsp extra
450 g/1 lb fettuccine
freshly grated nutmeg
salt and pepper
50 g/2 oz/½ cup freshly grated
   Parmesan cheese, plus extra to
   serve

*fettuccine*

*nutmeg*

*Parmesan cheese*

**1** Place the butter and 150 ml/5 fl oz/⅔ cup cream in a heavy saucepan, bring to the boil and simmer for 1 minute until slightly thickened.

**2** Cook the fettuccine in plenty of boiling salted water according to the manufacturer's instructions, but for 2 minutes' less time. The pasta should still be a little firm.

**3** Drain very well and turn into the pan with the cream sauce.

**4** Place on the heat and turn the pasta in the sauce to coat.

**5** Add the extra 60 ml/4 tbsp cream, the cheese, salt and pepper to taste and a little grated nutmeg. Toss until well coated and heated through. Serve immediately with extra grated Parmesan cheese.

# Spaghetti Olio e Aglio

This is another classic recipe from Rome. A quick and filling dish, originally the food of the poor involving nothing more than pasta, garlic and olive oil, but now fast becoming fashionable.

## Serves 4

INGREDIENTS
2 garlic cloves
30 ml/2 tbsp fresh parsley
100 ml/4 fl oz/½ cup olive oil
450 g/1 lb spaghetti
salt and pepper

*spaghetti*

*olive oil*

*parsley*

*garlic*

**1** Finely chop the garlic.

**2** Chop the parsley roughly.

**3** Heat the olive oil in a medium saucepan and add the garlic and a pinch of salt. Cook gently, stirring all the time, until golden. If the garlic becomes too brown, it will taste bitter.

**4** Meanwhile cook the spaghetti in plenty of boiling salted water according to the manufacturer's instructions until *al dente*. Drain well.

**5** Toss with the warm – not sizzling – garlic and oil and add plenty of black pepper and the parsley. Serve immediately.

# Double Tomato Tagliatelle

Sun-dried tomatoes add pungency to this dish, while the grilled fresh tomatoes add bite.

*Serves 4*

INGREDIENTS
45 ml/3 tbsp olive oil
1 garlic clove, crushed
1 small onion, chopped
50 ml/2 fl oz/¼ cup dry white wine
6 sun-dried tomatoes, chopped
30 ml/2 tbsp chopped fresh parsley
50 g/2 oz/½ cup stoned black
  olives, halved
450 g/1 lb fresh tagliatelle
4 tomatoes, halved
Parmesan cheese, to serve
salt and freshly ground black pepper

*parsley*

*garlic clove*

*tomatoes*

*sun-dried*
*tomatoes*

*tagliatelle*
*dry white*
*wine*

*onion*
*black*
*olives*

*Parmesan*
*cheese*

## COOK'S TIP

It is essential to buy Parmesan in a piece for this dish. Find a good source – fresh Parmesan should not be unacceptably hard – and shave or grate it yourself. The flavour will be much more intense than that of the ready-grated product.

**1** Heat 30 ml/2 tbsp of the oil in a pan. Add the garlic and onion and cook for 2–3 minutes, stirring occasionally. Add the wine, sun-dried tomatoes and the parsley. Cook for 2 minutes. Stir in the black olives.

**2** Bring a large pan of salted water to the boil. Add the fresh tagliatelle and cook for 2–3 minutes until just tender. Preheat the grill.

**3** Put the tomatoes on a tray and brush with the remaining oil. Grill for 3–4 minutes.

**4** Drain the pasta, return it to the pan and toss with the sauce. Serve with the grilled tomatoes, freshly ground black pepper and shavings of Parmesan.

# Spaghetti with Black Olive and Mushroom Sauce

A rich pungent sauce topped with sweet cherry tomatoes.

### Serves 4

INGREDIENTS
15 ml/1 tbsp olive oil
1 garlic clove, chopped
225 g/8 oz mushrooms, chopped
150 g/5 oz/generous ½ cup black
    olives, pitted
30 ml/2 tbsp chopped fresh parsley
1 fresh red chilli, seeded and chopped
450 g/1 lb spaghetti
225 g/8 oz cherry tomatoes
slivers of Parmesan cheese, to serve
    (optional)

*garlic*

*mushrooms*

*red chillies*

*cherry tomatoes*

*black olives*

*spaghetti*

*parsley*

**1** Heat the oil in a large pan. Add the garlic and cook for 1 minute. Add the mushrooms, cover, and cook over a medium heat for 5 minutes.

**2** Place the mushrooms in a blender or food processor with the olives, parsley and red chilli. Blend until smooth.

**3** Cook the pasta following the instructions on the side of the packet until *al dente*. Drain well and return to the pan. Add the olive mixture and toss together until the pasta is well coated. Cover and keep warm.

**4** Heat an ungreased frying pan and shake the cherry tomatoes around until they start to split (about 2–3 minutes). Serve the pasta topped with the tomatoes and garnished with slivers of Parmesan, if liked.

# Spinach and Ricotta Conchiglie

Large pasta shells are designed to hold a variety of delicious stuffings. Few are more pleasing than this mixture of chopped spinach and ricotta cheese.

## COOK'S TIP
Choose a large saucepan when cooking pasta and give it an occasional stir to prevent shapes from sticking together. If passata is not available, use a can of chopped tomatoes, sieved and puréed.

*Serves 4*

INGREDIENTS
350 g/12 oz large conchiglie
450 ml/¾ pint/scant 2 cups passata or
  tomato pulp
275 g/10 oz frozen chopped spinach,
  defrosted
50 g/2 oz crustless white bread,
  crumbled
120 ml/4 fl oz/½ cup milk
45 ml/3 tbsp olive oil
250 g/8 oz/2¼ cups Ricotta cheese
pinch of nutmeg
1 garlic clove, crushed
15 ml/1 tbsp olive oil
2.5 ml/½ tsp black olive paste
  (optional)
25 g/1 oz/¼ cup freshly grated
  Parmesan cheese
25 g/1 oz/2 tbsp pine nuts
salt and freshly ground black pepper

*olive paste*

*Ricotta cheese*

*pine nuts*

*garlic*

*spinach*          *conchiglie*

**1** Bring a large saucepan of salted water to the boil. Toss in the pasta and cook according to the directions on the packet. Refresh under cold water, drain and reserve until needed.

**2** Pour the passata or tomato pulp into a nylon sieve over a bowl and strain to thicken. Place the spinach in another sieve and press out any excess liquid with the back of a spoon.

**3** Place the bread, milk and oil in a food processor and combine. Add the spinach and Ricotta and season with salt, pepper and nutmeg.

**4** Combine the passata with the garlic, olive oil and olive paste if using. Spread the sauce evenly over the bottom of an ovenproof dish.

**5** Spoon the spinach mixture into a piping bag fitted with a large plain nozzle and fill the pasta shapes (alternatively fill with a spoon). Arrange the pasta shapes over the sauce.

**6** Preheat a moderate grill. Heat the pasta through in a microwave oven at high power (100%) for 4 minutes. Scatter with Parmesan cheese and pine nuts, and finish under the grill to brown the cheese.

# Pasta with Pesto Sauce

Don't stint on the fresh basil – this is the most wonderful sauce in the world! There are now good fresh pesto sauces in the chilled cabinets of large supermarkets. They taste completely different from the pesto sold in jars.

## Serves 4

INGREDIENTS
2 garlic cloves
salt and pepper
50 g/2 oz/½ cup pine nuts
50 g/2 oz/1 cup fresh basil leaves
150 ml/5 fl oz/⅔ cup olive oil (not extra-virgin as it is too strong)
50 g/2 oz/4 tbsp unsalted butter, softened
60 ml/4 tbsp freshly grated Parmesan cheese
450 g/1 lb spaghetti

*olive oil*

*spaghetti*

*pine nuts*

*Parmesan cheese*

*basil*

**1** Peel the garlic and process in a food processor with a little salt and the pine nuts until broken up. Add the basil leaves and continue mixing to a paste.

**2** Gradually add the olive oil, little by little, until the mixture is creamy and thick.

**3** Beat in the butter and season with pepper. Beat in the cheese. (Alternatively, you can make the pesto by hand using a pestle and mortar.)

**4** Store the pesto in a jar (with a layer of olive oil on top to exclude the air) in the fridge until needed.

**5** Cook the pasta in plenty of boiling salted water according to the manufacturer's instructions. Drain well.

## COOK'S TIP

A good pesto can be made using
parsley instead of basil and walnuts
instead of pine nuts. To make it go
further, add a spoonful or two of
fromage frais. 'Red' pesto includes
sun-dried tomato paste and pounded
roasted red peppers.

**6** Toss the pasta with half the pesto
and serve in warm bowls with the
remaining pesto spooned on top.

# Pasta Shells with Tomatoes and Rocket

This pretty-coloured pasta dish relies for its success on rocket, a tasty salad green. Available in large supermarkets, it is a leaf easily grown in the garden or in a window box. Rocket has a slightly peppery taste.

*Serves 4*

INGREDIENTS
450 g/1 lb/4 cups pasta shells
salt and pepper
450 g/1 lb ripe cherry tomatoes
45 ml/3 tbsp olive oil
Parmesan cheese, to serve
75 g/3 oz fresh rocket

*olive oil*

*pasta shells*

*cherry tomatoes*

*Parmesan cheese*

*rocket (arugula)*

**1** Cook the pasta in plenty of boiling salted water according to the manufacturer's instructions. Drain well.

**2** Halve the tomatoes. Trim, wash and dry the rocket.

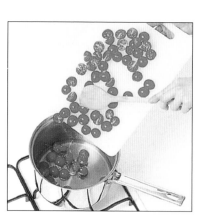

**3** Heat the oil in a large saucepan, add the tomatoes and cook for barely 1 minute. The tomatoes should only just heat through and not disintegrate.

**4** Shave the Parmesan cheese using a rotary vegetable peeler.

**5** Add the pasta, then the rocket. Carefully stir to mix and heat through. Season well with salt and freshly ground black pepper. Serve immediately with plenty of shaved Parmesan cheese.

# Oriental Vegetable Noodles

Thin Italian egg pasta is a good alternative to Oriental egg noodles; use it fresh or dried.

*Serves 6*

INGREDIENTS
500 g/1¼ lb thin tagliarini
1 red onion
115 g/4 oz shitake mushrooms
45 ml/3 tbsp sesame oil
45 ml/3 tbsp dark soy sauce
15 ml/1 tbsp balsamic vinegar
10 ml/2 tsp caster sugar
5 ml/1 tsp salt
celery leaves, to garnish

*tagliarini*

*shitake mushrooms*

*red onion*

*balsamic vinegar*

*soy sauce*

**1** Boil the tagliarini in a large pan of salted boiling water, following the instructions on the pack.

**2** Thinly slice the red onion and the mushrooms, using a sharp knife.

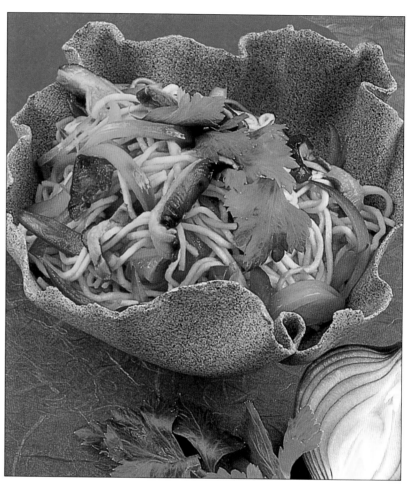

**3** Heat the wok, then add 15 ml/1 tbsp of the sesame oil. When the oil is hot, stir-fry the onion and mushrooms for 2 minutes.

**4** Drain the tagliarini, then add to the wok with the soy sauce, balsamic vinegar, sugar and salt. Stir-fry for 1 minute, then add the remaining sesame oil, and serve garnished with celery leaves.

# Singapore Noodles

A delicious supper dish with a stunning mix of flavours and textures.

### Serves 4

INGREDIENTS
225 g/8 oz dried egg noodles
45 ml/3 tbsp groundnut oil
1 onion, chopped
2.5 cm/1 in piece fresh root
   ginger, finely chopped
1 garlic clove, finely chopped
15 ml/1 tbsp Madras
   curry powder
2.5 ml/½ tsp salt
115 g/4 oz cooked chicken or
   pork, finely shredded
115 g/4 oz cooked peeled prawns
115 g/4 oz Chinese cabbage
   leaves, shredded
115 g/4 oz beansprouts
60 ml/4 tbsp chicken stock
15-30 ml/1-2 tbsp dark soy sauce
1-2 fresh red chillies, seeded
   and finely shredded
4 spring onions, finely shredded

*beansprouts*

*Chinese cabbage*

*noodles*

*ginger*

*curry powder*

*chicken*

*dark soy sauce*

*onion*

*stock*

*red chillies*

*spring onions*

*groundnut oil*

*prawns*

**1** Cook the noodles according to the packet instructions. Rinse thoroughly under cold water and drain well. Toss in 15 ml/1 tbsp of the oil and set aside.

**2** Heat a wok until hot, add the remaining oil and swirl it around. Add the onion, ginger and garlic and stir-fry for about 2 minutes.

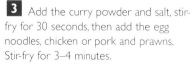

**3** Add the curry powder and salt, stir-fry for 30 seconds, then add the egg noodles, chicken or pork and prawns. Stir-fry for 3–4 minutes.

**4** Add the Chinese cabbage and beansprouts and stir-fry for 1–2 minutes. Sprinkle in the stock and soy sauce to taste and toss well until evenly mixed. Serve at once, garnished with the shredded red chillies and spring onions.

# Kedgeree with French Beans and Mushrooms

Crunchy French beans and mushrooms are the star ingredients in this vegetarian version of an old favourite.

## Serves 2

INGREDIENTS

115 g/4 oz/⁵/₄ cup basmati rice
3 eggs
175 g/6 oz French beans, trimmed
50 g/2 oz/¹/₄ cup butter
1 onion, finely chopped
225 g/8 oz brown cap mushrooms, quartered
30 ml/2 tbsp single cream
15 ml/1 tbsp chopped fresh parsley

single cream    brown cap mushrooms    parsley

onion

butter

French beans

eggs

basmati rice

**1** Wash the rice several times under cold running water. Drain thoroughly. Bring a pan of water to the boil, add the rice and cook for 10–12 minutes until tender. Drain thoroughly.

**2** Meanwhile, half fill a second pan with water, add the eggs and bring to the boil. Simmer for 8 minutes. Drain the eggs, cool under cold water, then remove the shells.

**3** While the eggs are cooking, cook the French beans in boiling water for 5 minutes. Drain, refresh under cold running water, then drain again.

**4** Melt the butter in a large frying pan. Add the onion and mushrooms. Cook for 2–3 minutes over a moderate heat.

**5** Add the French beans and rice to the onion mixture. Stir lightly to mix. Cook for 2 minutes. Cut the hard-boiled eggs in wedges and add them to the pan.

**6** Stir in the cream and parsley, taking care not to break up the eggs. Reheat the kedgeree, but do not allow it to boil. Serve at once.

# Mixed Rice Noodles

A delicious noodle dish made extra special by adding avocado and garnishing with prawns.

*Serves 4*

INGREDIENTS

15 ml/1 tbsp sunflower oil
2.5 cm/1 in piece root ginger, peeled
  and grated
2 cloves garlic, crushed
45 ml/3 tbsp dark soy sauce
225 g/8 oz peas, thawed if frozen
450 g/1 lb rice noodles
450 g/1 lb fresh spinach, coarse
  stalks removed
30 ml/2 tbsp smooth peanut butter
30 ml/2 tbsp tahini
150 ml/¼ pint/⅔ cup milk
1 ripe avocado, peeled and stoned
roasted peanuts and peeled prawns,
  to garnish

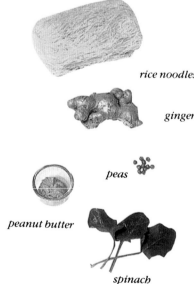

*rice noodles*

*ginger*

*peas*

*peanut butter*

*spinach*

**1** Heat the wok, then add the oil. When the oil is hot, stir-fry the ginger and garlic for 30 seconds. Add 15 ml/1 tbsp of the soy sauce and 150 ml/¼ pint/⅔ cup boiling water.

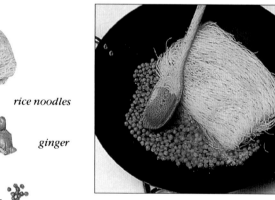

**2** Add the peas and noodles, then cook for 3 minutes. Stir in the spinach. Remove the vegetables and noodles, drain and keep warm.

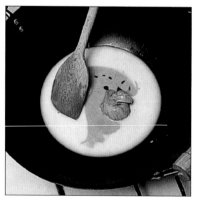

**3** Stir the peanut butter, remaining soy sauce, tahini and milk together in the wok, and simmer for 1 minute.

**4** Add the vegetables and noodles, slice in the avocado and toss together. Serve piled on individual plates. Spoon some sauce over each portion and garnish with peanuts and prawns.

# Capellini with Rocket, Mangetout and Pine Nuts

A light but filling pasta dish with the added pepperiness of fresh rocket.

*Serves 4*

INGREDIENTS
250 g/9 oz capellini or angel-hair pasta
225 g/8 oz mangetout
175 g/6 oz rocket
50 g/2 oz/¼ cup pine nuts, roasted
30 ml/2 tbsp Parmesan cheese, finely
  grated (optional)
30 ml/2 tbsp olive oil (optional)

*rocket*

*Parmesan*

*pine nuts*

*capellini*

*mangetout*

**1** Cook the capellini or angel-hair pasta following the instructions on the side of the packet until *al dente*.

**2** Meanwhile, carefully top and tail the mangetout.

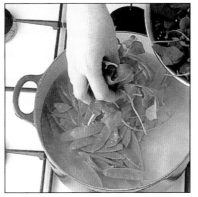

**3** As soon as the pasta is cooked, drop in the rocket and mangetout. Drain immediately.

**4** Toss the pasta with the roasted pine nuts, and Parmesan and olive oil if using. Serve at once.

## COOK'S TIP
Olive oil and Parmesan are optional as they obviously raise the fat content.

# Thai Fried Rice

This hot and spicy dish is easy to prepare and makes a meal in itself.

## Serves 4

INGREDIENTS

225 g/8 oz Thai jasmine rice
45 ml/3 tbsp vegetable oil
1 onion, chopped
1 small red pepper, seeded and
  cut into 2 cm/¾ in cubes
350 g/12 oz skinless and boneless
  chicken breasts, cut into 2 cm/
  ¾ in cubes
1 garlic clove, crushed
15 ml/1 tbsp mild curry paste
2.5 ml/½ tsp paprika
2.5 ml/½ tsp ground turmeric
30 ml/2 tbsp Thai fish sauce
  (*nam pla*)
2 eggs, beaten
salt and ground black pepper
fried basil leaves, to garnish

## VARIATION

Add 50 g/2 oz frozen peas to the chicken in step 3, if you wish.

**1** Put the rice in a sieve and wash well under cold running water. Put the rice in a heavy-based pan with 1.5 litres/2½ pints/6¼ cups boiling water. Return to the boil, then simmer, uncovered, for 8–10 minutes; drain well. Spread out the grains on a tray and leave to cool.

**2** Heat a wok until hot, add 30ml/ 2 tbsp of the oil and swirl it around. Add the onion and red pepper and stir-fry for 1 minute.

**3** Add the chicken, garlic, curry paste and spices and stir-fry for 2–3 minutes.

**4** Reduce the heat to medium, add the cooled rice, fish sauce and seasoning. Stir-fry for 2–3 minutes until the rice is very hot.

**5** Make a well in the centre of the rice and add the remaining oil. When hot, add the beaten eggs, leave to cook for about 2 minutes until lightly set, then stir into the rice.

**6** Scatter over the fried basil leaves and serve at once.

# Caramelized Apples

A sweet, sticky dessert which is very quickly made,
and usually very quickly eaten!

*Serves 4*

INGREDIENTS
675 g/1½ lb dessert apples
115 g/4 oz/½ cup unsalted butter
25 g/1 oz fresh white breadcrumbs
50 g/2 oz/½ cup ground almonds
rind of 2 lemons, finely grated
60 ml/4 tbsp golden syrup
60 ml/4 tbsp thick Greek yogurt,
     to serve

*lemon*

*golden syrup*

*ground almonds*

*apple*

**1** Peel and core the apples.

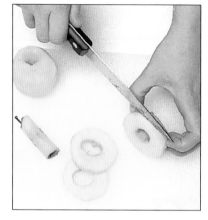

**2** Carefully cut the apples into 1 cm/
½ in-thick rings.

**3** Heat the wok, then add the butter.
When the butter has melted, add the
apple rings and stir-fry for 4 minutes until
golden and tender. Remove from the
wok, reserving the butter. Add the
breadcrumbs to the hot butter and stir-
fry for 1 minute.

**4** Stir in the ground almonds and lemon
rind and stir-fry for a further 3 minutes,
stirring constantly. Sprinkle the
breadcrumb mix over the apples, then
drizzle warmed golden syrup over the
top. Serve with thick Greek yogurt.

# Fruit Kebabs with Chocolate and Marshmallow Fondue

**Children love these treats – and with supervision they can help to make them.**

*Serves 4*

2 bananas
2 kiwi fruit
12 strawberries
15 ml/1 tbsp melted butter
15 ml/1 tbsp lemon juice
5 ml/1 tsp ground cinnamon

FOR THE FONDUE
225 g/8 oz plain chocolate
100 ml/4 fl oz/½ cup single cream
8 marshmallows
2.5 ml/½ tsp vanilla essence

*plain chocolate*

*bananas*

*vanilla essence*

*lemon juice*

*ground cinnamon*

*melted butter*

*single cream*

*marshmallows*

*kiwi fruit*

*strawberries*

**1** Peel the bananas and cut each into six thick chunks. Peel the kiwi fruit thinly and quarter them. Thread the bananas, kiwi fruit and strawberries on to four wooden or bamboo skewers.

**2** Mix together the butter, lemon juice and cinnamon and brush the mixture over the fruits.

**3** For the fondue, place the chocolate, cream and marshmallows in a small pan and heat gently on the barbecue, without boiling, stirring until the mixture has melted and is smooth.

**4** Cook the kebabs on the barbecue for 2–3 minutes, turning once, or until golden. Stir the vanilla essence into the fondue and serve it with the kebabs.

# Quick Apricot Blender Whip

One of the quickest desserts you could make – and also one of the prettiest.

*Serves 4*

INGREDIENTS
400 g/14 oz can apricot halves in juice
15 ml/1 tbsp Grand Marnier or brandy
175 g/6 oz/¾ cup Greek yogurt
30 ml/2 tbsp flaked almonds

*Greek yogurt*

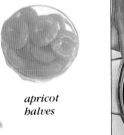

*Grand Marnier*

*apricot halves*

*flaked almonds*

**1** Drain the juice from the apricots and place the fruit and liqueur in a blender or food processor.

**2** Process the apricots until smooth.

**3** Spoon the fruit purée and yogurt in alternate spoonfuls into four tall glasses or glass dishes, swirling them together slightly to give a marbled effect.

**4** Lightly toast the almonds until they are golden. Let them cool slightly and then sprinkle them on top.

## COOK'S TIP

For an even lighter dessert, use low-fat instead of Greek yogurt, and, if you prefer to omit the liqueur, add a little of the fruit juice from the can.

# Chocolate Mousse on the Loose

**Super-light, dark, creamy and delicious; the chocolate mousse is always popular and should maintain a high profile on any dessert menu.**

*Serves 4*

INGREDIENTS
200 g/7 oz best quality plain
   chocolate, plus extra for flaking
3 eggs
30 ml/2 tbsp dark rum or whisky
50 g/2 oz/¼ cup caster sugar
300 ml/½ pint/1¼ cups
   whipping cream
icing sugar, for dusting

*plain chocolate*

*whipping cream*

*eggs*

*caster sugar*

**1** Break the chocolate into a bowl, stand over a saucepan of simmering water and melt. Separate the egg whites into a large mixing bowl, remove the chocolate from the heat and stir in the egg yolks and alcohol.

**2** Whisk the egg whites until firm, gradually add the sugar and whisk until stiff peaks form.

**3** Whip the cream to a dropping consistency and set aside until required.

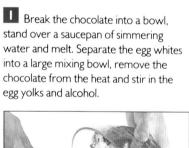

**4** Give the egg whites a final beating with a rubber spatula, add the chocolate and fold all the ingredients together gently, retaining as much air as possible.

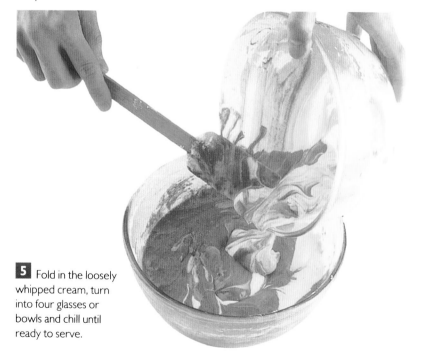

**5** Fold in the loosely whipped cream, turn into four glasses or bowls and chill until ready to serve.

## COOK'S TIP

It is a false economy to use inexpensive chocolate. Choose the best quality dark chocolate you can find and enjoy it!

**6** Decorate with flaked chocolate and dust with icing sugar.

# Brazilian Coffee Bananas

Rich, lavish and sinful-looking, this dessert
takes only about 2 minutes to make!

### Serves 4

INGREDIENTS
4 small ripe bananas
15 ml/1 tbsp instant coffee granules or
   powder
15 ml/1 tbsp hot water
30 ml/2 tbsp dark muscovado sugar
250 g/9 oz/1⅛ cups Greek yogurt
15 ml/1 tbsp toasted flaked almonds

*Greek yogurt*

*bananas*

*flaked almonds*

*instant coffee*

*dark muscovado sugar*

**1** Peel and slice one banana and mash
the remaining three with a fork.

**2** Dissolve the coffee in the hot water
and stir into the mashed bananas.

**3** Spoon a little of the mashed banana
mixture into four serving dishes and
sprinkle with sugar. Top with a spoonful
of yogurt, then repeat until all the
ingredients are used up.

**4** Swirl the last layer of yogurt for a
marbled effect. Finish with a few banana
slices and flaked almonds. Serve cold. Best
eaten within about an hour of making.

## VARIATION

For a special occasion, add a dash –
just a dash – of dark rum or brandy
to the bananas for extra richness.
15 ml/1 tbsp of rum or brandy adds
about 30 calories.

# Barbecued Strawberry Croissants

A deliciously simple, sinful dessert, which is like eating warm cream cakes!

*Serves 4*

4 croissants
115 g/4 oz/$^1\!/_2$ cup ricotta cheese
115 g/4 oz/$^1\!/_2$ cup strawberry
   conserve or jam

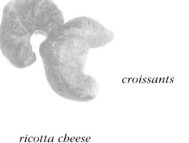

*croissants*

*ricotta cheese*

*strawberry conserve*

**1** Split the croissants in half and open them out on a board.

**2** Spread the bottom half of each croissant with ricotta cheese.

**3** Top with a generous spoonful of strawberry conserve and replace the top half of the croissant.

**4** Place the croissants on a hot barbecue and cook for 2–3 minutes, turning once.

## Cook's Tip

As an alternative to croissants, try fresh scones or muffins, toasted on the barbecue.

# Mixed Melon Salad with Wild Strawberries

Ice-cold melon is a delicious way to end a meal. Here several varieties are combined with strongly flavoured wild or woodland strawberries. If wild berries are not available, use ordinary strawberries or raspberries.

*Serves 4*

INGREDIENTS
1 cantaloupe or charentais melon
1 galia melon
900 g/2 lb water melon
175 g/6 oz wild strawberries
4 sprigs fresh mint

COOK'S TIP
Ripe melons should give slightly when pressed at the base, and should give off a fruity, melony scent. Buy carefully if you plan to use the fruit on the day.

*wild strawberries*

*galia melon*

*mint*

*cantaloupe melon*

*water melon*

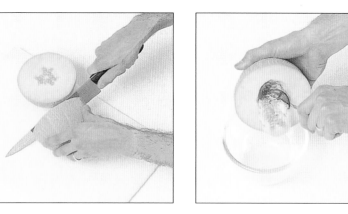

**1** Halve the cantaloupe, galia and water melons.

**2** Remove the seeds from the cantaloupe and galia with a spoon.

With a melon scoop, take out as many balls as you can from all 3 melons. Combine in a large bowl and refrigerate.

**4** Add the wild strawberries and turn out into 4 stemmed glass dishes.

**5** Decorate with sprigs of mint.

# Pineapple Wedges with Rum Butter Glaze

Fresh pineapple is even more full of flavour when grilled; this spiced rum glaze makes it into a very special dessert.

*Serves 4*

1 medium pineapple
30 ml/2 tbsp dark muscovado
  sugar
5 ml/1 tsp ground ginger
60 ml/4 tbsp melted butter
30 ml/2 tbsp dark rum

*pineapple*

*melted butter*

*dark muscovado sugar*

*ground ginger*          *dark rum*

**1** With a large, sharp knife, cut the pineapple lengthways into four wedges. Cut out and discard the centre core.

**2** Cut between the flesh and skin, to release the flesh, but leave the skin in place. Slice the flesh across, into chunks.

**3** Push a bamboo skewer lengthways through each wedge and into the stalk, to hold the chunks in place.

**4** Mix together the sugar, ginger, melted butter and rum and brush over the pineapple. Cook the wedges on a hot barbecue for 3–4 minutes; pour the remaining glaze over the top and serve.

## COOK'S TIP

For an easier version, simply cut off the skin and then slice the whole pineapple into thick slices and cook as above.

# Nectarines with Marzipan and Mascarpone

A luscious dessert that no one can resist – dieters may like to use low-fat soft cheese or ricotta instead of mascarpone.

## Serves 4

4 firm, ripe nectarines or
  peaches
75 g/3 oz marzipan
75 g/3 oz/5 tbsp mascarpone
  cheese
3 macaroon biscuits, crushed

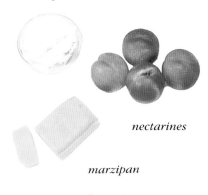

*mascarpone cheese*

*nectarines*

*marzipan*

*macaroon biscuits*

**1** Cut the nectarines or peaches in half, removing the stones.

**2** Cut the marzipan into eight pieces and press one piece into the stone cavity of each nectarine half.

## COOK'S TIP

Either peaches or nectarines can be used for this recipe. If the stone does not pull out easily when you halve the fruit, use a small, sharp knife to cut around it.

**3** Spoon the mascarpone on top. Sprinkle the crushed macaroons over the mascarpone.

**4** Place the half-fruits on a hot barbecue for 3–5 minutes, until they are hot and the mascarpone starts to melt.

# Prune and Orange Pots

A simple, storecupboard dessert, made in minutes.
It can be served straight away, but it's best chilled
for about half an hour before serving.

*Serves 4*

### INGREDIENTS
225 g/8 oz/1 ½ cups ready-to-eat dried
   prunes
150 ml/¼ pint/⅔ cup orange juice
225 g/8 oz/1 cup low-fat natural
   yogurt
shreds of orange rind, to decorate

*orange juice*

*natural yogurt*

*orange rind*

*prunes*

**1** Remove the stones from the prunes and roughly chop them. Place them in a pan with the orange juice.

**2** Bring the juice to the boil, stirring. Reduce the heat, cover and leave to simmer for 5 minutes, until the prunes are tender and the liquid is reduced by half.

**3** Remove from the heat, allow to cool slightly and then beat well with a wooden spoon, until the fruit breaks down to a rough purée.

**4** Transfer mixture to a bowl. Stir in the yogurt, swirling the yogurt and fruit purée together lightly, to give an attractive marbled effect.

**5** Spoon the mixture into stemmed glasses or individual dishes, smoothing the tops.

**6** Top each pot with a few shreds of orange rind, to decorate. Chill before serving.

## VARIATION

This dessert can also be made with other ready-to-eat dried fruit, such as apricots or peaches. For a special occasion, add a dash of brandy or Cointreau with the yogurt.

# Mango and Coconut Stir-fry

Choose a ripe mango for this recipe. If you buy one that is a little under-ripe, leave it in a warm place for a day or two before using.

### *Serves 4*

INGREDIENTS
¼ coconut
1 large, ripe mango
juice of 2 limes
rind of 2 limes, finely grated
15 ml/1 tbsp sunflower oil
15 g/½ oz/1 tbsp butter
30 ml/1½ tbsp clear honey
crème fraîche, to serve

*coconut*

*mango*

*honey*

*lime*

**1** Prepare the coconut flakes by draining the milk from the coconut and peeling the flesh with a vegetable peeler.

**2** Peel the mango. Cut the stone out of the middle of the fruit. Cut each half of the mango into slices.

## COOK'S TIP

Because of the delicate taste of desserts, always make sure your wok has been scrupulously cleaned so there is no transference of flavours – a garlicky mango isn't quite the effect you want to achieve!

**3** Place the mango slices in a bowl and pour over the lime juice and rind, to marinate them.

**4** Meanwhile, heat the wok, then add 10 ml/2 tsp of the oil. When the oil is hot, add the butter. When the butter has melted, stir in the coconut flakes and stir-fry for 1–2 minutes until the coconut is golden brown. Remove and drain on kitchen towels. Wipe out the wok. Strain the mango slices, reserving the juice.

**5** Heat the wok and add the remaining oil. When the oil is hot, add the mango and stir-fry for 1–2 minutes, then add the juice and allow to bubble and reduce for 1 minute. Then stir in the honey, sprinkle on the coconut flakes and serve with crème fraîche.

# Apples and Raspberries in Rose Pouchong Syrup

Inspiration for this dessert stems from the fact that the apple and the raspberry belong to the rose family. The subtle flavours are shared here in an infusion of rose-scented tea.

*Serves 4*

INGREDIENTS
5 ml/1 tsp rose pouchong tea
5 ml/1 tsp rose water (optional)
50 g/2 oz/¼ cup sugar
5 ml/1 tsp lemon juice
5 dessert apples
175 g/6 oz/1½ cups fresh raspberries

*tea*

*apples*

*sugar*

*raspberries*

COOK'S TIP
If fresh raspberries are out of season, use the same weight of frozen fruit or a 400 g/14 oz can of well drained fruit.

**1** Warm a large tea pot. Add the rose pouchong tea and 900 ml/1½ pints/3¾ cups of boiling water together with the rose water, if using. Allow to stand and infuse for 4 minutes.

**2** Measure the sugar and lemon juice into a stainless steel saucepan. Strain in the tea and stir to dissolve the sugar.

**3** Peel and core the apples, then cut into quarters.

**4** Poach the apples in the syrup for about 5 minutes.

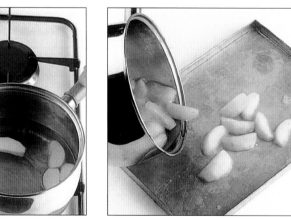

**5** Transfer the apples and syrup to a large metal tray and leave to cool to room temperature.

**6** Pour the cooled apples and syrup into a bowl, add the raspberries and mix to combine. Spoon into individual dishes or bowls and serve warm.

# Cherry Pancakes

These pancakes are virtually fat-free, and lower in calories and higher in fibre than traditional ones. Serve with a spoonful of natural yogurt or fromage frais.

*Serves 4*

INGREDIENTS
FOR THE PANCAKES
50 g/2 oz/½ cup plain flour
50 g/2 oz/⅓ cup plain wholemeal
   flour
pinch of salt
1 egg white
150 ml/¼ pint/⅔ cup skimmed milk
150 ml/¼ pint/⅔ cup water
a little oil for frying

FOR THE FILLING
425 g/15 oz can black cherries in juice
7.5 ml/1½ tsp arrowroot

*skimmed milk*

*wholemeal flour*

*plain flour*

*black cherries*

*arrowroot*          *egg*

**1** Sift the flours and salt into a bowl, adding any bran left in the sieve to the bowl at the end.

**2** Make a well in the centre of the flour and add the egg white. Gradually beat in the milk and water, whisking hard until all the liquid is incorporated and the batter is smooth and bubbly.

**3** Heat a non-stick pan with a small amount of oil until the pan is very hot. Pour in just enough batter to cover the base of the pan, swirling the pan to cover the base evenly.

**4** Cook until the pancake is set and golden, and then turn to cook the other side. Remove to a sheet of absorbent paper and then cook the remaining batter, to make about eight pancakes.

**5** Drain the cherries, reserving the juice. Blend about 30 ml/2 tbsp of the juice from the can of cherries with the arrowroot in a saucepan. Stir in the rest of the juice. Heat gently, stirring, until boiling. Stir over a moderate heat for about 2 minutes, until thickened and clear.

## COOK'S TIP

If fresh cherries are in season, cook them gently in enough apple juice just to cover them, and then thicken the juice with arrowroot as in Step 5.

The basic pancakes will freeze very successfully. Interleave them with non-stick or absorbent paper, overwrap them in polythene and seal. Freeze for up to six months. Thaw at room temperature.

**6** Add the cherries and stir until thoroughly heated. Spoon the cherries into the pancakes and fold them in quarters.

# INDEX